THE BRIDE'S TRUNK
A Story of War and Reconciliation

Ingrid Dixon

Cloudshill Press

Cheltenham and London, England

Cloudshill Press

Published by **Cloudshill Press**
Registered Office: 27 Old Gloucester Street, London WC1N 3AX United Kingdom

Book Layout © 2014 BookDesignTemplates.com

The Bride's Trunk/ Ingrid Dixon. -- 1st ed.
Paperback ISBN 978-0-9935080-2-8
Ebook ISBN 978-0-9935080-1-1

For my grandchildren

"Alles, was uns begegnet, läßt Spuren zurück. Alles trägt unmerklich zu unserer Bildung bei."

"Everything we encounter leaves traces behind. Everything contributes imperceptibly to our education."

—Johann Wolfgang von Goethe, Wilhelm Meisters Lehrjahre, 1795

"It is not enough to win a war; it is more important to organise the peace."

—Aristotle

COMMENTS ABOUT THE BRIDE'S TRUNK

An extraordinary narrative, pieced together from original documents, about a couple who were determined not to let war defeat them. Seventy years ago the British government passed a law allowing British men to marry German women, but little thought was given to the life that those German women would find, in the aftermath of the Second World War. This heart-warming tale brings alive childhood and adolescence in pre-war Germany, followed by a new life in the old enemy country.

Jackie Ashley, President of Lucy Cavendish College, University of Cambridge, and journalist

Scant attention has been paid to the 10,000 or so German women who married British soldiers at the end of the Second World War. In this often moving account, Ingrid Dixon traces the story of her own parents, one a former secretary for the German police, the other a British soldier from the Intelligence Corps, both of whom were caught up in the chaotic last months of the Third Reich and its immediate aftermath. Their story is carefully pieced together from personal and official documents, oral testimony and material objects, including the old trunk which survived the vicissitudes of war to carry the bride's worldly possessions to her new home in Liverpool.

Professor Peter Wilson, Chichele Professor of the History of War, University of Oxford

A gripping and moving story, with excellent illustrations, which really evokes time and place and is a sensitive treatment of the conflicting feelings associated with war.

Dr Philip Towle, Department of Politics and International Studies, University of Cambridge

CONTENTS

List of Illustrations

Foreword

Trunk   n. 1. The main stem of a tree as distinct from its branches and roots. 2. A person's or animal's body apart from the limbs and head. 3. The main part of any structure. **4. A large box with a hinged lid for transporting luggage, clothes etc.** *5. N. Amer. The luggage compartment of a motor car.   6. An elephant's elongated prehensile nose.   (Oxford English Reference Dictionary)*

German – Autokoffer (-), Reisekoffer (-)

The trunk is over a hundred years old. No clues indicate a firm of manufacturers or a city in which it was made. The craftsmen who added sturdy leather handles and clasps, who reinforced it with metal corners and tan leather trim, who lined it with green baize, are unknown. But beneath yellowing layers of crumbling paper labels which cling to its blistered dark surface, the initials "v. N." applied in black are just visible. Similar pieces of luggage stand forgotten in dusty attics all over Europe. Materially the trunk is unremarkable, an object of little value. In human terms, though, it tells a story, a thread linking three generations of two families across political, geographical and linguistic divides. During the course of the twentieth century the trunk has been taken over frontiers, seas and thresholds, dragged onto boats, trains, cars, trucks and horse-drawn carts. It has been packed in anger, despair, haste and hope, invested with expectations and fears as the events of the decades dictated its movements and shaped the lives of its owners.

The trunk was first acquired by Emil Rössler, my grandfather, from his employer, Georg Nellessen, in the early years of the 20th Century, and has now passed to me. In what follows I tell the story of its travels and of the people who owned it. Even as a small child I was aware of the trunk, a solid presence sitting in the corner of our home. It contained mundane objects: bed linen and tablecloths, fur hats and bundles of letters. Often, pushed against the wall of a bedroom, and covered by a worn blanket or bedspread, it was forgotten until called upon to serve its purpose as a piece of luggage. I only became curious as to its history and provenance as an adult, by which time many of those who could have narrated its story were no longer alive. But I have pieced it together, as told principally by Minny, my mother, who was born to Emil and his wife Berta in Germany 96 years ago. Others from both Germany and Britain have elaborated and corroborated the narrative. I owe them all a great debt.

Ingrid Dixon, 2016

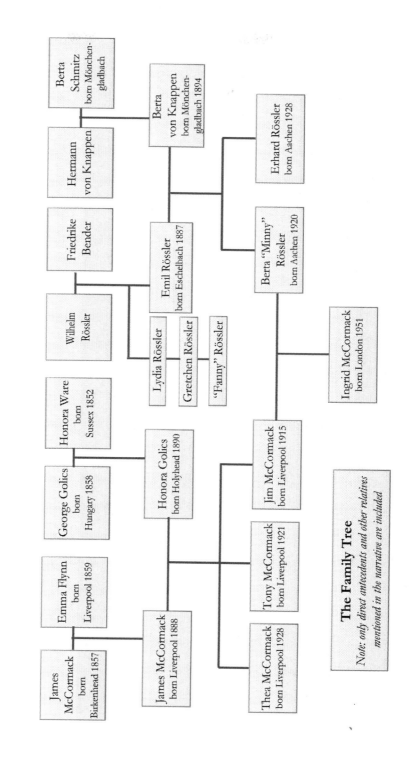

The Family Tree

Note: only direct antecedents and other relatives mentioned in the narrative are included

CHAPTER ONE

December 1946: England

Jim travels to Germany to collect Minny in early December 1946. Her family is living in sparsely furnished and cheerless rooms under the roof rafters of a rented house. Firewood can still be gathered in the nearby woods to feed the ancient blackened stove. Electricity and water supplies are intermittent.

Gut Klau, Buchweg, Aachen-Vaalserquartier. A group of farm buildings in a suburb of the ancient city of Aachen, once capital to Charlemagne's empire in the eighth century and reduced to a heap of smouldering ruins after bloody fighting between American and German troops in the autumn of 1944. Aachen is the first city on German soil taken by the Allies, of huge symbolic importance in Hitler's shattered dream of a thousand year Reich. It is now in the British Zone, one of four controlled by the governments in the alliance which defeated the Third Reich in May 1945. In the summer of 1946 the British occupiers have combined two existing states to create a new German state of Nordrhein-Westfalen, in a process they call "Operation Marriage".

As light is fading and the evening promises nothing more than a supper of leftover potatoes and some *Sauerkraut* obtained by bartering cigarettes, a knock comes on the door. Minny hears the murmur of voices in the hallway as Emil, her father, answers. "Come here please, Minny", he calls. At first she does not recognise Jim in civilian clothes, a "demob" suit, long heavy overcoat and sturdy leather shoes.

Jim in uniform

She has only ever seen him in British army uniform, as a soldier in one of the military units which occupied and administered the British Zone in Germany after the final capitulation in May 1945. He has all the necessary travel permits for the journey back to England. "But we need to leave tomorrow", explains Jim. His permit from the authorities to enter Germany from Holland expires the next morning and he must return over the border the following day. Will she go with him, leave her family and travel to an unfamiliar country where she will meet with hostility and incomprehension, where people speak a different language, where the privations will be similar to those she is currently experiencing? Months of preparation and uncertainty now culminate in one night in which to determine the course of her life.

How will her family fare without her? Daily life revolves around seeking food and fuel. Most transactions are still carried out by bartering. Large loaves of dark rye bread are available with food coupons. Notices appear pinned to buildings, announcing when and where deliveries of groceries are expected.

While Berta, her mother, talks to Jim, he eats the remains of their supper. Emil sits with Minny on the stairs, deliberating. No one tries to persuade her one way or the other. Her future depends on her decision. Emil is realistic and sets out the facts, assessing the situation from all points of view. She will be living in a country where she is regarded as the "enemy". She might be denied a return to Germany for many years. Was he as even-handed as Minny remembers? While he had come to enjoy Jim's company and thought him an honest man, Emil might be forgiven for trying to dissuade her, scarred by weeks in a British prisoner-of-war camp. Minny tries to imagine obstacles which might lie ahead, but one simple fact above all others sways her: she wants to be with Jim.

Emil helps pack her trunk, which has survived British and American bombs and bears the scuffs and dents of many journeys across combat zones in the death throes of the Third Reich. Now it will play a new role in accompanying Minny to an unknown future in an alien country. Emil carefully places a dress, in which Minny will marry, on top of sheets, tablecloths and linen embroidered with family initials. Fur stoles are added, as Berta has heard rumours that England is a chilly country and she must be prepared. On the top is laid a Persian rug in deep blues and purples, bought in the Middle East by Emil after the First World War, when he was a soldier in the Kaiser's forces. It depicts a paradise garden in which small plump birds peck at lush vegetation, fed by a flowing fountain. A green art deco clock from the twenties is pushed down the side; a small sculptured silver fox with one leg blown off is cushioned between clothes and a leather handbag. Everyone sleeps fitfully.

On a bitter grey December morning Minny departs with Jim. She is dressed in a coat made of American army blankets, sewn on a machine salvaged from the rubble of a bombed house, and dyed blue. Weak sunlight begins to break through the clouds. Emil, Berta and Minny's younger brother Erhard stand shivering at the front door as a Jeep draws up that is to drive them to the border with Holland, for the onward journey to a railway station where trains might be running to the coast. Travel papers are checked, the clasps of the trunk are secured and it is loaded. What is left to say? No photographic record of the event, no speeches, just a few tears. A brief embrace and they are gone.

In the aftermath of war, transport is unreliable, haphazard. From Aachen, they are taken to the Dutch border, a few short kilometres in distance, along roads pitted by bombing and littered with the twisted wreckage of conflict. Cables and wires have been temporarily strung along roads. As the Jeep lurches down the lane, precious permits allowing travel to Britain and marriage to a British citizen, which have been hidden deep in Minny's underwear for safety, scratch and are a reminder of the decision she has taken. She has never left Germany, the country of her birth, before, except for short excursions to neighbouring markets in nearby Holland and Belgium, for which only temporary passes were required. Nor has she ever seen a large expanse of ocean or travelled by sea.

The Jeep is driven by a friend of Minny's brother, who now has to return to Aachen. Jim has booked a taxi from the border to Maastricht, from where they hope to reach a railway station. By dusk, after several train journeys and a section in an ancient jolting bus, they reach the Hook of Holland and board a boat to Harwich. There are not yet regular scheduled ferry crossings from Holland to Britain; sailing times are still sporadic and unreliable, but a ship is due to leave.

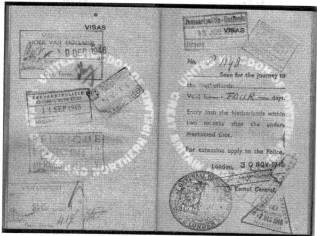

Jim's Passport - 'collecting' Minny

Jim's passport from that period survives. It shows a visa to enter Holland, and the multiple entry and exit stamps which document his journey from Harwich to the Hook of Holland, his travel through Holland to Aachen to collect Minny, and his return with her via Hook of Holland to Harwich on 9th December.

Porters haul the trunk aboard and place it beside wooden slatted seats, bleached by wind, rain and age. As the ship sets sail, it begins to rock and pitch. Jim has crossed the North Sea many times. In the 1930s, right up until 1939, he cycled around the flat lowlands of Belgium, Holland and France, taking holiday snaps of towns and villages shortly to be devastated by war. In preparation for the D-Day Allied invasion in June 1944, its aftermath and the final demise of Germany, he had trained with the British Army Intelligence Corps, and been based in locations in both Belgium and Holland before entering Germany as part of the forces occupying the defeated country. He speaks near-fluent Dutch and French, as well as German.

But for Minny, the experience of seasickness is new and unexpected. The remains of the simple rations of bread and cheese packed for the journey are untouched. Around them sit refugees and soldiers from many nations, wounded and displaced people, goods and animals, not to mention other prospective so–called "war brides".

At the time Minny is unaware of others in similar circumstances to herself. But the closing months of 1946 witness hundreds of German women travelling to Britain to marry soldiers they have met in the aftermath of the end of hostilities, when four conquering Allied nations occupied and administered Germany.

97   C.M. 53 (46).-

Marriages between British Servicemen and Foreigners.
(Previous Reference: W.M.(45)29th Conclusions, Minute 4.)

3. The Cabinet considered a memorandum by the Secretary of State for War (C.P. (46) 211) suggesting that some relaxation might now be made of the existing rules restricting marriages between British Servicemen and foreign women.

The Secretary of State for War said that it was proposed in his memorandum, with the concurrence of the Foreign Secretary, that the existing restrictions should now be relaxed to the extent of allowing marriages between Servicemen and foreign women (other than Germans and Japanese) if the local military commander considered that there were good reasons for, and no security objections against, the marriage; that marriages with German women should be authorised only in very special cases; and that the absolute ban on marriages with Japanese women should be maintained. It was his personal view that the time had now come when the restrictions on marriages with Germans could be further relaxed; but he wished to obtain further advice on the legal position and to consult the Commander-in-Chief on the security aspects of the matter before submitting definite proposals on this point to the Cabinet.

The Parliamentary Under-Secretary of State for Air said that the Air Ministry supported the recommendations made in C.P. (46) 211. They would have preferred that the discretion to authorise in exceptional cases marriages between British airmen and German women should be vested in the Air Ministry; but they were prepared, for the sake of uniformity, to agree that this discretion should be exercised by the Commander-in-Chief.

In discussion it was pointed out that the relaxations proposed by the Secretary of State for War would give rise to difficulties in various directions. The principal points made in the discussion were :—

(a) These relaxations would enable women of ex-enemy nationality to become British subjects. This would be contrasted with the Government's reluctance to confer British nationality on Allied nationals who had fought against the enemy during the war, often under British command. It would also be contrasted with the Government's refusal to accept the argument that a foreigner's marriage with a British woman gave him a right to prolong his residence in the United Kingdom.

(b) A German woman marrying a British soldier would acquire British nationality; but a British woman marrying a foreigner who had fought in one of the Allied Forces would in most cases lose her British nationality. This was a situation which would give rise to adverse comment. If marriages between British Servicemen and German women had to be allowed, could it be provided that the woman should not thereby acquire British nationality?

Cabinet Minutes 30th May 1946

The question of marriage between German citizens and members of the British Armed Forces begins to be considered and discussed in late 1945, and throughout 1946 and 1947. Control Commission records, British Cabinet records and Hansard Parliamentary reports document an ongoing debate, culminating in statements in July and August of 1946 in Parliament (see Historical Note 1). Decisions made relating to British military personnel are additionally complicated by differing legal requirements relating to marriage in Germany, where it is not normally legally binding unless those involved have undergone both civil and church ceremonies.

There appear to be myriad variations on the same issue. It is, after all, uncharted territory. What if for instance, a serving soldier had returned to Britain, leaving his fiancée in Germany, and she came to join him? Minny's case represents yet another permutation. Jim has returned to Britain as a serving soldier, but was immediately "de-mobbed" and so is no longer in active service. On the 1st August 1946 a statement is made by Mr Lawson, Secretary of State for War, in response to persistent questions on the subject from MPs.

"After careful consideration the Government have decided to relax the ban on marriages at present in force between British Servicemen and women of ex-enemy countries, other than Japanese. Local military commanders will be given authority to permit such marriages in cases where there is no security or other objection".

This is followed by a short discussion on the issue, and consequently groups of German women start arriving on British shores. On 8th October a subsequent question is asked in Parliament: how many women have travelled to Britain since the lifting of the ban? No answer is available since a record of numbers has not been kept.

As the ship sails through the night, acute nausea forces Minny to consider the wisdom of her decision. They speak little. But after the ship docks on a foggy cold morning in

Harwich, and they file down the swaying gangplank onto the chilly quayside, accompanied by their luggage, seasickness begins to subside. They present themselves at Customs Control, and Minny digs out documents, allowing entry into Britain and marriage to a British citizen, from their hiding place in her clothing. None of the papers survive today, but they stipulate that the marriage has to take place within a week of arrival. Another permit to remain in Britain for 7 days is issued. Jim acts as interpreter as Minny is questioned.

On the train to London as day dawns, immediate first impressions of England are formed. A combination of the stormy crossing and the intense emotion of the previous days has left Minny feeling dazed and nervous. People are speaking an unfamiliar language.

Yet she instantly begins to take in differences from the country she has left behind and asks Jim to explain the multiple chimney pots and chimney stacks on rows of terraced houses she observes, as they flash past the grimy train windows. In Germany, houses have one chimney pot at most. Jim describes rooms still heated with open fires, and adds that smoke emissions from thousands of chimneys in urban areas contribute to the formation of impenetrable "pea-souper" fogs.

As the train passes through the London suburbs and approaches Liverpool Street station, she observes that the women on the London streets wear considerable amounts of make-up and lipstick, and their clothing seems to be sparse and inadequate for the bitter winter weather. London is grey and damp. As in Germany, bomb damage is evident everywhere, rubble fills the streets, pavements and road surfaces remain unrepaired.

The final stage of the journey to her new home is by train from Euston Station to Liverpool, where Jim's parents have lived since before his birth in 1915, and where he spent his childhood. Liverpool is in the grip of such a thick dark fog, as described by Jim, that the driver of the taxi from the station is unable to make out the road ahead. In the darkness he stops the vehicle, so Jim gets out and walks ahead of the taxi with a lantern the driver has provided, to light the way.

As the car inches slowly forward, Minny is horrified. They are unable to find the right road. Doesn't he know where he lives, she thinks? They arrive at Lingfield Road, Broad Green, a road of modest semi-detached houses with small front gardens, where Jim's family are nervously assembled to greet her. It is the first house they have ever owned. The trunk is dragged up the path to the front door. Lights in the hallway illuminate their arrival as Jim pays the taxi driver and they enter.

In retrospect she is unable to say whether her initial reception is in any way representative of that of other war brides. She can only describe how she is received. If Jim's parents are feeling apprehension or bitterness, they do not show it. Memories not only of the Second, but also of the First World War are still fresh in the national and personal memory. Jim's uncle, Anthony Golics, had been killed in action in France on 29th September only weeks before the Armistice was declared in 1918.

Liverpool has been extensively bombed and bears many scars. Many of their neighbours and acquaintances have lost family members in the fighting and bombing. In private Jim and Nora have initially expressed dismay and even horror at their son's intention to marry a German girl. But now such misgivings must be put aside and notions of Germans as the "enemy" must somehow be overcome. They are gathered round the open fire in the dining room of Number 38 for initial introductions.

Minny has already studied photos of all her future family members. Her father-in-law, James McCormack, whose family originated in Ireland, fluently and elegantly welcomes her in her own native tongue. As a young man he had taught English in Moravia, part of the now defunct Austro-Hungarian Empire, and learned to speak German. During the Second World War, too old for active service, he has worked as a censor on letters from internees and German prisoners held in captivity on British soil.

He has intimate knowledge of Germany and its people, and in the aftermath of war is using his extensive French and German language skills in the export department of a Liverpool company of food exporters, specialising in tinned goods. He and Minny have already exchanged many letters. In his meticulous spidery handwriting he has written to her in eloquent German of family members, of how they are eagerly anticipating her arrival, of how he hopes she has devoted time to improving her English, signing himself *Vati* – "Dad".

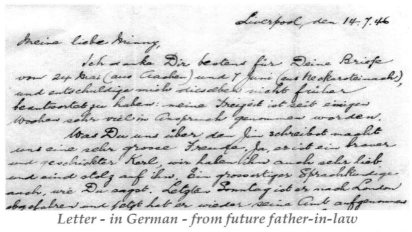

Letter - in German - from future father-in-law

His wife, Honora Anna, *née* Golics, always known to family members as "Nora", is half Hungarian, but has been raised in Wales, on the island of Anglesey, the third of five children. Her father, a miller by trade, had emigrated from rural Hungary in the 1880s to work in the flourishing flour mills of Holyhead, and married Honora Smith *née* Ware, in whose house he initially lodged in the early days after his arrival. Minny will later describe her new mother-in-law as "my dearest friend". In the early years of the century, Nora's father - Hungarian George - a sister and two brothers had moved to Canada, but she had stayed in Britain.

Since the announcement of Minny and Jim's engagement in the first weeks of 1946, she too has been sending encouraging letters. "I'm sure you'll soon settle down in England", she has written, "It's not such a bad place. I wish you and Jim every happiness and as long as you can make him happy, I can't wish for anything else". She is short with wavy greying hair and a kindly face and will later tell Minny of her premonition, upon learning of his posting to Germany in 1945, that Jim would bring home a German bride.

Letter from future mother-in-law

Jim's younger sister Thea, shortened from Dorothea, is eighteen and at Art College in Liverpool, intending to be a fashion designer. Thea and Jim have a close bond and in the days to come she forms a rapport with Minny, in spite of the language barrier. Minny finds her friendly and glamorous, and is surprised to see her smoking! Minny will have to wait to meet Jim's younger brother Tony, as he will not return until Christmas. On Minny's first evening in England, she is served poached white fish and shown to a chilly bedroom, while Jim spends the night on the sofa downstairs.

Minny and Thea

On the following morning, the trunk is lifted upstairs and, as Nora helps Minny unpack, surprise is expressed on both sides! How is it that a girl from the "vanquished" nation has managed to bring several changes of clothing and such a quantity of bed and table linen? How has it survived unscathed? Minny soon discovers that German square pillow cases do not fit rectangular British pillows! The British do not sleep under feather-filled duvets, which mould themselves to the shape of the body, but under sheets and hard blankets, which let in draughts! She is not expecting the simplicity of their lives, as representatives of the "Conquerors". Washing is done in an annexe adjacent to the kitchen, containing tub and mangle. Basic commodities are in short supply as strict food and coal rationing is still in operation in Britain, as in Germany. But in late 1946, prior to their meeting, Jim and Nora have been sending food parcels to Minny and her parents in Aachen, through charitable organisations in Britain dedicated to helping the German nation back on to its feet. Victor Gollancz has founded one such organisation, named "Save Europe Now". So she is not expecting the deprivations and shortages immediately evident in a household with a steady but modest income.

Later in the day Minny observes Liverpool in grey daylight as she travels by tram with Jim to organise the wedding, which is to take place in the Register Office. She is struck by the still extensive evidence of German bombing, and by the poverty of many of those out on the streets. Children scurry around without shoes. Women hurry to shops, heads wrapped in shawls against the bitter cold. Minny understands little of the formal arrangements as the date is set for 13th December, Jim's 31st birthday and less than a week after his prospective wife has arrived.

Minny marries Jim wearing the simple dark patterned dress she has carried in the trunk. Their wedding photo shows them flanked by Jim senior and Nora, but Paul Butcher, who acts as best man and witness, is missing from the image.

Minny has difficulty in following the language of the ceremony, so at appropriate points, when a response is required, Jim whispers, "*Sag Ja!*" (say yes). The officiating Registrar speaks in the accent of Liverpool, making comprehension even more difficult! Finally, Jim says "*Jetzt sind wir verheiratet!*" (Now we are married).

As soon as it is developed, the photo will be sent to parents and brother in Aachen. After the ceremony, the family walks to the Adelphi Hotel, a prestigious Edwardian landmark, to celebrate with a meal of roast turkey; eating out in such a way is still not possible in Germany. As Jim has to return to work in London immediately after Christmas, a honeymoon will have to be delayed. Married life has begun.

Nora, Jim, Minny and Jim senior, 13th December 1946

CHAPTER TWO

1920 – 1930: Childhood

Minny was born in 1920 in Aachen, a city with multiple names, positioned uneasily at the point where three languages touch: the *Dreiländereck* – corner of three countries. To historians it is Aix-la-Chapelle, where peace treaties ending European wars were signed in 1668 and 1748.

Charlemagne, king of the Franks, attracted by dense forests rich in game, and steaming sulphurous medicinal springs, made the location his capital in the eighth century. To architectural historians, the city is the site of his octagonal palace chapel reflected in the French name, modelled by the king on the church of San Vitale in Ravenna in Italy and embellished with Roman marble columns transported as spolia from that city. The Dutch call the city Aken, and speculate that the forebears of painter Hieronymous Bosch, whose true family name was van Aken, originated there. But the city was in Germany, so to its citizens it was known by the only name proclaimed on the railway station – Aachen – the initial double "a" guaranteeing first place in the index of most world atlases. The name was said to come from the old German word for water - *Ahha*. Hot pungent-smelling springs bubbling up from deep in the ground were discovered by Roman soldiers, who maintained that bathing in them eased aches and pains.

The proximity of Belgium and Holland ensured that food, customs and local dialect words of the three countries were bound up with each other: pedlars and mobile grocers called at Minny's house with horse and cart, selling huge, round Dutch cheeses, and the heavy, curved wooden clogs that her father wore to dig the vegetable garden. On the cobbled market place in front of the town hall, vats of pickled herrings and mussels from Holland stood alongside mounds of Dutch and Belgian fruit and vegetables, while Belgian soldiers in the streets shouted in French, their presence dictated by the terms of the Versailles Treaty ending the First World War. Even the local speciality, *Printen,* chewy spiced oblong biscuits, were first made by a Dutchman, who pressed (*prenten* in Dutch) the dough into moulds before it was baked.

Kaisersruh

A traveller on the straight road which struck out north of the city up a steep hill to the mining town of Würselen, might, if glancing in the right direction, glimpse a pair of iron gates. Beyond, a short tree-lined drive led to an elegant three-storey stone-clad house in a classical style, with later neo-baroque addition, dating from the early nineteenth century, and an entrance porch framed with Doric columns. The house was surrounded by an informally laid-out park, orchards, outbuildings and stables, lakes stocked with goldfish and large carp, and a kitchen garden screened by hedges. Adjacent farms supplied dairy products and meat. The estate of Kaisersruh was owned by the Nellessen family, prosperous German landowners and local cloth manufacturers who employed Minny's father as chauffeur, and provided the use of a small two-storey stone house, standing in the shadow of their own, on his marriage to Minny's mother in 1918. Georg Nellessen had moved to the estate in 1899, carrying out alterations in 1905 to the main house and outbuildings.

Georg Nellessen

In flashes of early memory Minny is sitting in a pram in its gardens, squealing as she tries to catch and bite into a newly-hatched chick that her father has brought from the henhouse and placed in her lap. Then she and her mother are struggling up the hill from the city with shopping in a crocheted string bag and she has to walk because a wheel has fallen off the old metal push-chair. Or she is running in the park, where a weathered wooden plaque nailed to an oak tree explains the origin of the name Kaisersruh – Emperor's Rest.

Tsar Alexander of Russia had stopped to rest under the tree during a walk in 1818, when the estate was owned by a Baron von Fisenne, who was granted permission by the Tsar to name the estate in commemoration of the event. As a player on the world stage, Aachen had hosted informal talks when the signatories of the Treaty of Vienna, which had ended the Napoleonic wars three years earlier, met to discuss its terms and implications; the Tsar attended as the representative of his empire. A small railway halt nearby bore the name of the estate.

Minny's parents shared a widely held view that the crippling reparations and military constraints imposed on Germany by the conditions of the Treaty of Versailles in 1919 represented deep injustices. But having survived the First World War, they were hopeful for a better future, living by the motto *sparen fürs Alter* – save for one's old age. She was their first child, christened Berta Wilhelmine, a family name that reminded of the Kaiser who had recently abdicated and was in exile in Holland with his family. To avoid confusion she became known as Minny, as her mother also bore the name Berta. Their lives were ruled by the twin virtues of hard work and thrift.

Her father Emil grew vegetables, raised poultry and rabbits for the table, drove his wealthy employer, Georg Nellessen, on hunting trips and holidays to Italy and had duties tied up with the management and running of the estate.

Emil Rössler

Emil as a military driver

In the attic, where washing swung on wet days, sat several large trunks. One, edged in brown leather with metal corners, accompanied Emil as he drove his employers on their European travels, to the Italian lakes and beyond. Luggage was strapped to the back of the car with heavy broad leather restraints. The trunk that had come into Emil's possession bore the initials "v. N", the additional "v" a vestige from the previous century when the Nellessen family name still bore the aristocratic prefix "von".

Emil (centre) and Army colleagues in the Middle East

Another huge domed trunk had returned intact after use by Emil during the First World War, and was cavernous enough for concealment when Minny played hide and seek. It housed dusty Arab headdresses, and bags of coins from Palestine and Russia, where Emil had driven trucks in the First World War, clothes worn when camping in the desert with Bedouins and faded photographs of two unmarried sisters, Tante (Aunt) Gretchen and Tante Fanny, who had been a Protestant missionary in South America. Bundles of postcards written in the old *Suetterlin* German script and bearing faded unfamiliar stamps were wrapped in a scarf he had used to protect nose and mouth from the desert sand. He told tales of childhood near Heidelberg and of his forebears: Protestant pastors, and shepherds who drove flocks between Germany and the French border.

Emil's father Wilhelm, with a grandchild

Emil's mother Friedrike, with a grandchild

After an apprenticeship in the fledgling car industry with Daimler-Benz in Mannheim, Emil worked in the garage of the von Luttitz family near Aachen, where his future wife Berta von Knappen, Minny's mother, was employed as lady's maid and children's governess in the household. Berta described their first encounter as *Liebe auf den ersten Blick* – love at first sight.

Verarmter Adel was the succinct description she applied to her family: impoverished nobility. They could boast the aristocratic "von" in their surname but nothing remained of land or property that might have been. Her father, Minny's grandfather Hermann von Knappen, whose monogram "v. K" was stitched into every piece of table and bed linen, had the title of *Spinnmeister* – master in spinning – and specialised in overseeing spinning in cloth factories around Mönchengladbach and Stolberg, north of Aachen, where a traditional cloth industry had flourished since the early nineteenth century. He supplied the family with large unwieldy bales of cloth, which were cut and sewn into clothes at Kaisersruh on a groaning treadle machine by a visiting seamstress who exchanged gossip with Berta and made dolls' clothes for Minny from the offcuts.

Berta with her father Hermann von Knappen

Minny aged 4

Minny's early childhood was a lull before the storm, precariously balanced between the horrors of the First World War and the abyss to come. Unlike much of the population of the 1920s, her father had secure employment and housing, a cushion from the rampant inflation of 1923 and from many of the economic and social hardships endured by the working classes in the cities. Food was in abundance on the estate, unwanted furniture from the large estate house was provided to furnish their more modest quarters.

First Day at School

A photograph shows Minny on her first day at school, aged six, a stiff bow in her wiry auburn hair, socks slipping defiantly down her legs, clutching the large black slate given to mark the occasion. Every morning, together with children from neighbouring farms, who were also her childhood playmates, she trudged the six kilometres up the hill to Würselen, where brown coal, or lignite, was extracted from deep mines. Rucksack-style satchels contained wooden pencil boxes and slates, but if a girl wore the style intended for boys, which had longer flaps, this indicated hand-me-downs in a family strapped for cash. On dark winter mornings, wrapped in heavy green *loden* cloaks, they carried small metal lanterns, each enclosing a tiny candle, to light the way.

In the schoolroom Minny came face to face with the economic realities of the 1920s. Many pupils lacked proper shoes – wearing clogs instead – their clothes inadequate, their diet meagre. The bundles of outgrown clothes taken to school to be distributed amongst classmates reinforced the supposition of wealth. Pupils who could afford to buy textbooks shared them with those who could not. Sitting in rows of boys on one side and girls, wearing aprons over their dresses, on the other, they scratched letters on slates with styluses and erased them with sponges suspended on a short string. At that time German children were still taught the *Suetterlin* script, where an "e" resembles an "n". Good work was rewarded with cards depicting Catholic Saints.

The schoolmaster was frequently far from sober, enforcing discipline with the aid of a stick and falling asleep by the large stove that warmed the room in cold weather. Above the stove swung a line with drying outdoor clothes that soon began to steam and release the rich smells of the farmyards from which pupils had set off.

In a staunchly Catholic area, Minny's family were Protestants, so at her parents' request she withdrew from the Catholic religious instruction. But she still participated in the many Catholic festivals that punctuated the year. Each 11th November on the feast of St. Martin children processed around neighbouring houses carrying small hollowed-out turnip lanterns, begging for sweets. St. Martin was revered for having given up his cloak to a beggar, his deeds commemorated in a traditional song sung before a meal of roast goose with red cabbage. Before the rigours of Lent, extravagant *Karneval* celebrations were staged, when clubs, associations and political parties decorated floats which wound in raucous parades through the ancient streets of the city to the cheers of masked onlookers in fancy dress. Bands played, sketches were performed, political masters were satirised, paper flags and hats rained down from the wagons.

Released from school, Minny would check a list scribbled on paper attached to her clothing with a safety-pin, reminding her to collect bread from the bakery before walking home for lunch, which was served at twelve noon every day; to miss the deadline was a mortal sin. Daily existence on the estate was regulated by the need to produce, harvest, prepare and store food. Minny's mother ran the household with ordered, punctual efficiency, where everyone had their allotted place and tasks.

Out of school, Minny's life consisted of unending monotonous chores. There were vegetables to pick and scrub, carrots, potatoes, beans, cabbage, *kohlrabi* and herbs to chop, shred and grate, soups to stir, dough and pastry to knead, fruit to peel, stone, puree, preserve and bottle. For the leaner winter months, they filled glass and blue-glazed earthenware jars with cucumbers, cherries, plums, jams and pickles and stacked them in orderly rows on slatted shelves in the attic. Apples and pears were layered in straw, beans and *Sauerkraut* stored in a cupboard under the stairs in huge earthenware vats whose water had to be changed periodically.

Emil returned from hunting trips laden with hare, venison, pheasant and boar, which were turned into pâtés, pies and stews. On baking days, bread, cakes and flans were carried to the adjacent farm to be cooked in their cavernous oven. From the farm dairy next door, rich pungent unpasteurised milk was hauled home in a metal churn, and stored in the *Fliegenschrank* (fly cupboard) – a small wooden cupboard with a wire-mesh front – under the stairs, as there was no cold storage.

Minny polished shoes lined up in rows on the stairs, shovelled coal and slag into buckets in the yard and dragged them to the kitchen ready to fuel the stove. Sacks of grain were hauled to a nearby mill for grinding. Not all jobs were unpleasant however. A donkey named *Treu* (faithful), lived in one of the stables, where she fed him in winter; in summer she led him out onto the meadow to chew grass. In return he could be hitched to a small wooden cart for transport.

Berta's instructions echo in her head across the decades. "Don't forget to close the gate, Minny", she called as metal pails from the first-floor laundry were hauled down to the grass where bedsheets were spread and sprinkled with water to be bleached by the sun. Then they were dragged back to the kitchen to be rinsed again before being pegged on lines strung across meadows shared with neighbours. If Minny protested at the endless chores, she was reminded of her good fortune in being fed and clothed when many went without basics. In defiance, she deliberately left gates open and watched as cows and horses chewed up the sheets.

The monotony of daily life was relieved by visits to the city of Aachen or as guests in the adjacent house of Herr and Frau Nellessen, to celebrate the year's landmarks. Estate employees were invited to a cold buffet harvest supper, while at Christmas a scented tree from the woods stood in the billiard room, dangerously lit with candles held in metal clips. It was a solemn affair. The lady of the house, Delphine Nellessen, a tall stately Dutchwoman whose only child, a son, had died of diphtheria, distributed gifts which she had carefully chosen and wrapped, or even made herself. Laid out in readiness on a table, they were presented to each person attending: an embroidered waistcoat, a tiny fragile piece of glass or china, a supple leather purse, silver sugar tongs or a carved wooden sphere which split open to reveal a ball of delicate thread.

Children recited poetry and Christmas carols were sung. For formal dinners, Minny's father was enlisted in calculating the amounts of food necessary and in skilfully arranging pieces of carved meat and game on huge platters before they were carried out to be served at a banquet.

The Nellessen's life was chiefly devoted to leisure. Laundry was collected every week and returned laundered, as Frau Nellessen disliked seeing it drying. Minny's family and theirs coexisted side by side; she lived on the fringe of a world whose privileges she could observe and occasionally be allowed to participate in.

Aachen was a centre for equestrian events. Guests of the Nellessens attending the horse trials stabled their horses in the outbuildings, and estate workers were given tickets to watch show jumping or dressage events. Riding in an open cart to the showground, they sat enthralled at the foot of the grandstand, and watched as members of the Dutch royal family took their seats. Here Minny glimpsed British, German and Dutch aristocrats, members of the royal houses of Europe, the privileged, wealthy and titled adorned with silk, furs and feathers.

The Kaisersruh servants, Minny far right

To the inhabitants of Aachen, their illustrious king Charlemagne was "*Karl der Grosse*" – Charles the Great - his name and deeds woven into the fabric of the buildings and streets. But he was also the butt of local jokes and school playground chants and was caricatured on the *Karneval* floats. Facts were mixed with myths; it was claimed that he couldn't read or write, and that Irish monks who fostered learning at his court were responsible for the high incidence of red hair in the region. It was even claimed that *Printen* had cured him of a stomach ailment, centuries before they were first produced. Intrinsic to German national pride and consciousness, and crowned by the Pope as head of the Holy Roman Empire on Christmas Day 800, he was the first ruler to preside over a disparate group of peoples that later became Germany. The octagonal chapel he had commissioned, the first of its type north of the Alps, to which the gothic choir was added in the mid-fourteenth century, dominated the city skyline and housed his remains in a sumptuous medieval shrine surrounded by towering marble arches.

Aachen Cathedral around 1900

Generations of Germanic monarchs had been crowned in the *Dom* (cathedral) on Charlemagne's throne; even Dürer had sketched the building in 1520 and painted an imaginary portrait of Charlemagne after his visit. Minny used the cathedral as a landmark to navigate by in the city. Flower sellers clustered around its buttressed walls. A butcher's shop in the shadow of the apse offered her samples of salami to taste, while purchases were wrapped in waxed paper.

In the city streets she learned where to hold her breath and quicken her pace to avoid pungent sulphurous smells given off by steaming springs. The city was founded by Roman legionaries who bathed in the hot, evil-smelling water bubbling from the ground. Along with other Aacheners, Minny's mother firmly believed in the water's restorative powers and at the colonnaded *Elisenbrunnen* (Elise's fountain) sampled the water, from metal cups hanging on chains around a marble fountain.

The existence of spa waters entitled Aachen to use the prefix *Bad* (spa) in its name, attracting visitors to hotels where they could bathe in the waters. The most illustrious of these had been Napoleon's wife, the Empress Josephine, in 1804 when the city was under French rule.

In the suburb of Burtscheid, the emerging springs were incorporated into public fountains, from which the local women filled pails and carried the readily available, free hot water home for cleaning, washing clothes and bathing children. In 1850 a certain Paul Julius Reuter arranged for carrier pigeons to deliver news on to the roof of his Aachen house from Brussels: a forerunner of the worldwide Reuter news agency.

A trip into the city ended with a visit to grandparents von Knappen, who, before retiring to Königswinter on the Rhine in 1925, lived in a small apartment up several narrow flights of stairs, where Minny and her mother delivered cakes baked at home or vegetables from the garden. The small girl was expected to sit quietly while the adults talked.

The walk from Kaisersruh to the city and back was several kilometres. As an alternative, they walked to the nearby village of Haaren and then took a tram, but this cost money which could be put to better uses.

Erhard Rössler in his pram

Minny was eight when brother Erhard was born, in a nursing home in the Jakobstrasse, and babysitting was added to her chores. The Nellessen family agreed to alter the layout of the house to provide extra space. The kitchen, previously on the first floor, was rebuilt on the ground floor in the *Sattelkammer* (saddle room) – a redundant space remaining from when horses had been kept in the stables, and the occupant of the house had been a coachman on the estate – giving a spacious family living area. Storage cupboards which had formerly housed leather riding tack lined one wall, and held sacks of rice, flour, raisins and pulses that were delivered by a mobile grocer by horse and cart. By the stove stood an old deckchair where Emil sat to read the newspapers. The stove stood on feet; cats and dogs crept under it for warmth. A brown leather sofa and other unwanted furniture were acquired from the larger estate house next door.

Saturday was *Putztag* (cleaning day). The room was edged with a strip of concrete which Minny had to polish with red paste, and a huge square of linoleum in the centre also required buffing – her most hated tasks. On a central wooden table she learned to knead yeast dough for sweet fruit flans, gutted fish and game, sliced up sausages and ham which had arrived in the post from Westphalia.

In the first-floor sitting room, warmed by the traditional *Kachelofen* (stove decorated with coloured glazed tiles), Emil displayed his collection of Dutch oil paintings, acquired through accompanying Herr Nellessen to auctions and bidding for items himself. Berta often questioned the number of paintings brought home. He considered them an investment for the future; they would have been, had they survived. In this room, grandmother von Knappen, having strode from the city in buttoned leather boots and dark voluminous skirts, expected to be entertained to afternoon coffee and cake. Her forthright views and involvement in family life were not welcomed by Minny's parents. Education, she felt, was a commodity wasted on girls, who should learn to cook and keep house, or might aspire to waitressing in a cafe. Thankfully her advice was largely ignored. Every week she walked across the border into Holland, to market in Vaals, from where she brought long triangular paper cones of sweets. She took walks around the park in the company of Herr Nellessen, with whom she seemed to have a rapport, and returned to the city on foot the following day after staying the night. Her daughter was relieved at her departure.

Holidays were only for the rich leisured classes such as the Nellessens, but Minny and her mother, before the arrival of a brother, took the train to the Black Forest, where Tante Fanny, Emil's sister, had been sent by the Protestant mission who trained her as a nursing sister. There she worked with families living in traditional wooden houses accommodating people and animals in the same living space. While Minny explored the green sloping meadows in the sunshine, Berta and Tante Fanny worked with the farmers' wives in interiors blackened with centuries of wood smoke, where sausages, hams and meat hung to be smoked by the fire, and box beds were built into the walls, screened by curtains. There was no proper sanitation or running water, and they slept on the floor.

Tante Fanny (second from left)

Tante Fanny always dressed in the long grey and white nun's habit of her order, and devoted her life to helping the poor. Her fiancé had been attacked and killed by a shark in

waters off the coast of Surinam in Central America, a former
Dutch colony, where she had cared for leprosy patients on a
missionary settlement. She never married. In her apartment in
Heidelberg a smelly squawking parrot was a reminder of those
days. Tante Fanny immediately donated the clothing and food,
which Berta had brought in large baskets, to the less fortunate.
From her, Minny learned to dry flowers and herbs for use in
teas, herbal medicines and cooking.

Minny's parents' lives entailed hard work, an existence
closely bound up with the land and the rhythm of the seasons.
Spring flowers concealed glistening coloured Easter eggs in the
annual hunt. At local farms, children crouched in the hay and
watched damp foals and calves being born. Ducks wandered
from the lakes in the park to the kitchen door with their young,
to be fed scraps. In autumn, Herr Nellessen allowed children
from Würselen to gather edible chestnuts fallen from trees
lining the ancient avenues which crossed his land. They
gathered conkers into huge sacks to take on hunts. As
swallows perched in rows on telephone wires, predictions were
made as to the length and severity of the coming winter, when
children skated on frozen lakes, or tobogganed on the slopes of
the estate. Unbeknown to them, those days were numbered.
Their isolated, cosseted life outside the city had shielded them
from the political events, economic catastrophes and upheavals
of the decade.

In 1929, Belgian troops that had occupied the city since the
Treaty of Versailles in 1919 were withdrawn amid much
rejoicing. The following year, 1930, President Hindenburg
visited Aachen and posed for photographs in a dark suit and
tall black hat. That year, aged ten, Minny took an exam to enter
secondary school in Aachen, the only pupil from her primary
school to pass. As she entered a new phase, Germany too was
to embark on a decade whose outcome could not be foreseen.

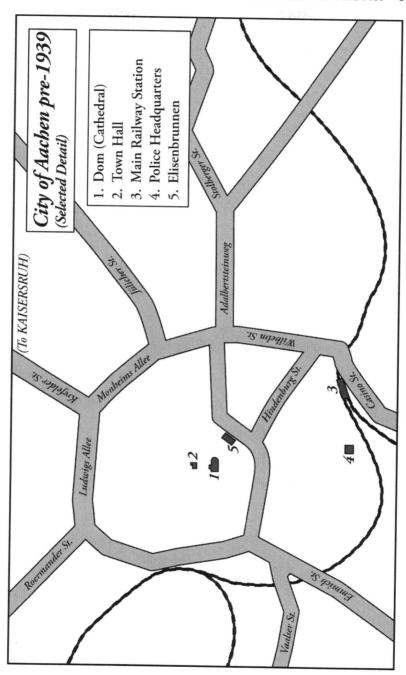

City of Aachen pre-1939
(Selected Detail)

1. Dom (Cathedral)
2. Town Hall
3. Main Railway Station
4. Police Headquarters
5. Elisenbrunnen

1930 – 1939: Adolescence

Minny should not have been surprised at gaining entry to secondary school. Her mother, Berta, dressed in best tailored suit with fox stole, matching hat and jewelled brooch, accompanied her to the interview to make the right impression. Secondary schooling was only available to those who could afford fees. Her parents ignored the advice of grandparents, who considered money spent on girls' education to be wasted. But Berta, who wore her long fine light brown hair wound into a tight bun, kept in place with slim hairpins, spoke precisely and with authority, and was not a woman to be trifled with.

Minny had to get up even earlier than when at primary school, walk to the small railway halt near Kaisersruh and take the train to the *Nordbahnhof* (north railway station), from where she reached the *Mädchenmittelschule* (girls' middle school) in the Beeckstrasse on foot. School finished in the early afternoon, with no midday meal provided. Emil arranged a stopover with an acquaintance from the First World War, Herr König, who ran a butcher's business in the city and supplied the Nellessen household. She could then join in afternoon activities such as sport, without having to return home for lunch.

Grandmother von Knappen had not offered help. After the death of her husband in retirement on the Rhine at Königswinter, she had moved back to Aachen and lived with her son, Onkel Willi, a customs officer stationed on the border with neighbouring Belgium, and his wife Tante Hedwig.

Teachers in dark dresses with white collars and cuffs taught new subjects - history, geography and biology. Proximity to French-speaking areas ensured the teaching of French as a first foreign language. English was introduced to the timetable soon afterwards, and Minny eventually had to choose between the two, opting to discontinue English. *"Ich komme doch nie nach England"*, she explained to her parents – "I'll never get to visit England!" *"Es hat keinen Zweck"* – "There's no point!" These words would haunt her for decades.

Years later, when wrestling with English verbs and pronunciation she was reminded of all the reasons why she had opted to give it up. French seemed so much more accessible to tongue and mind. Language teaching focused mostly on grammar with little consideration of cultural context, but French was more tangible and relevant. Many local dialect words had French origins, as the Rhineland had been occupied by the French in Napoleonic times – the word for "duvet" in the Rhineland is *Plumeau* or *Plümo* – alluding to the French for feather. French was spoken in parts of adjacent Belgium, but Britain and its inhabitants remained remote and irrelevant.

In 1933, when Hitler came to power, Minny was 13; this was a momentous event in European history but not in her life, which continued to centre on the mundane, everyday matters of home and school. The new regime progressively introduced measures to ensure their ideology was taught in schools alongside material traditionally included in the curriculum.

1930s School Book with Suetterlin Script

Minny was engrossed in learning the poetry of Romantic poets Heine, Eichendorff and Mörike and reading the plays of Kleist, Goethe and Schiller, as well as being impressed with the need to keep the German race pure. She longed to see the treasures of the Pergamon Museum in Berlin, brought to Germany by nineteenth century archaeologists, and begged her father for support in disputes with Berta over unfashionable clothes passed on from aunts and cousins, and shapeless socks crocheted by Emil's sisters, but was told to consider herself fortunate. As her birthday was in February when snow often lay on the ground, Berta conceded a delayed whole-day birthday party in the summer for school friends, who lived in apartments in the city and for whom a visit to the country was out of the ordinary. Feasting on creamy chicken fricassée, mushrooms and rice, followed by strawberry picking or a walk, and home-made plum flan with whipped cream, they gossiped about boys and longed for more freedom. Adolescence is in some essentials a similar experience for everyone, and there was no reason to think hers unusual.

She recalls her parents returning from voting, carrying small buttons proclaiming *Ja!* – an exhortation used by the Nazi Party in elections and referenda. Years later she was perplexed when reading or hearing about events she had lived through yet was unable to recall. But her parents avoided extremes and neither welcomed and actively supported the Nazi regime, nor opposed it. Political analysis was not in their nature and there was little discussion as to the rights or wrongs of the new government or the events which led to its establishment, such as the burning of the Reichstag. It is said that inhabitants of the Rhineland are by nature accommodating and accepting of whatever political system is imposed, keeping heads down until a storm passes. Allegiances go only skin deep and can be changed quickly. If her parents commented on politics in the early 1930s, Minny was not present or did not heed its significance. As a teenager, she admits, she lacked the maturity or insight to interpret happenings or recognise signs which in retrospect had signalled what was to come.

In the early years of the Third Reich, perceptions of the new government and its leader were overwhelmingly positive. They addressed the issues of homelessness and unemployment in Aachen and the surrounding region. Newspapers reported improvements in the economy and infrastructure of the country. The building of a new motorway system was providing jobs for thousands. Before the NSDAP (*Nationalsozialistische Deutsche Arbeiterpartei,* National Socialist German Workers' Party or 'Nazi' Party) came to power, scuffles had broken out in the streets between rival political factions; Minny's mother had warned her to run fast, should she inadvertently witness street clashes. Now, by contrast, the city seemed more ordered and stable; the turbulent years of the Weimar Republic, with successive of heads of state, were followed by those when one party and its leader seemed to be establishing control.

Minny, Berta and Erhard, mid-1930s

Excursions of any sort were welcome diversions in Minny's strict and tightly controlled upbringing. On occasion she was permitted to visit the Aachen theatre, where from 1934 onwards Herbert von Karajan, later to acquire world renown, had been appointed to conduct operatic concerts.

The Nazi Party fostered participation in sports and outdoor activities which were bound up with a love of the countryside and a sense of communal wellbeing. Minny joined a handball club and played for a local team. Her parents, though, often vetoed participation in school outings, claiming their isolated location outside the city made transport problematical. Realising that she was being exposed to new and unknown influences, they insisted she was indispensable at home, especially in busy summer and autumn months when vegetables and fruits needed harvesting and bottling. She rarely questioned their authority.

At school, though, she was automatically enrolled in the BDM (*Bund Deutscher Mädel*), the female wing of the Hitler Youth, whose uniform was a blue skirt, white blouse and dark scarf. Although teachers and local BDM leaders encouraged the singing of political songs or discussions on national socialism on school hiking or camping trips and visits to youth hostels in the nearby wooded Eifel area, the ideology for Minny was secondary to enjoyment of the outdoors. The *Horst Wessel Lied* (Horst Wessel Song) became a symbol of the Nazi ethos, an alternative unofficial national anthem.

A whole generation was being schooled in ideas radically different from those of their parents. In many households parents kept their views private, in case children should inadvertently and innocently let slip casual remarks, betraying their families' indifference or even opposition to the regime.

BDM girls in Olympic Stadium, Berlin, May 1937

As Minny approached the end of formal schooling in 1936 and expressed an intention to enter the pharmaceutical industry, the changing political climate does not seem to have affected her discussions with her parents. In Germany, dispensing chemists were, and still are, distinct from shops selling toiletries. As a child she was drawn by the cool tranquil interiors where ingredients for medicines were stored in labelled wooden drawers and compartments before being weighed on huge gleaming scales and mixed into powders for waiting customers. But entry into this and other commercial spheres and the securing of jobs at that time came primarily through connections or word of mouth.

The government appeared to be tackling employment for the male population, but women were discouraged from work outside the home; the Nazi Party was actively fostering the traditional female roles of *Kinder, Küche, Kirche*, (children, kitchen, church) with special emphasis on the first two. Eventually women would be awarded an Iron Cross medal for giving birth to four or more children.

When Minny acquired the *Mittlere Reife* (school certificate at age 16), most of her fellow pupils aspired to further training courses or apprenticeships, but only few achieved their goal. She was one of the lucky ones. Emil was acquainted with the director of the *Kommerzbank*, who knew Herr Boosfeld, director of the Geilenkirchen and Boosfeld firm of pharmaceutical wholesalers in Aachen. After the bank director's secretary had been entertained to coffee at Kaisersruh and discussed Minny's aspirations, an interview was arranged at the company, which she attended with her mother, and in the spring of 1936 she was selected as one of four apprentices (the only girl) to start three years of training.

Acceptance in an apprenticeship scheme in the volatile economic and political climate was considered an achievement, promising a security and a future which was at that point not envisaged as being under threat. Soon after she joined the company (known as "Geibo"), the Rhineland was remilitarised and on 28th March Hitler visited Cologne, about 75 kilometres from Aachen. In accordance with conditions laid down in the Treaty of Versailles of 1919 and agreed in the subsequent Locarno Treaties, no German troops had been stationed in the Rhineland.

Now the ban was lifted and the event celebrated. An employee of the company where Minny was an apprentice, who was a high-ranking party member - *Ein hohes Tier in der Partei,* as they were disparagingly referred to - arranged for a group, which included Minny, to travel in an open truck to the rally in Cologne. Parking on the edge of the city, they joined streams of people eagerly converging on foot on the centre, waiting for what seemed hours in an immense crowd of people for Hitler's arrival. A brief fleeting glance left her disappointed and deflated after the engineered excitement and build-up, when it was impressed upon participants what a privilege it was to have been present.

Cologne Newspaper 1936

For the occasion Minny was allowed to buy a so-called *Berchtesgadener* cardigan, a knitted green Tirolean jacket named after Hitler's mountain retreat in Bavaria where he received dignitaries and withdrew with his most trusted circle.

In the summer of 1936 as they listened to radio broadcasts reporting on the Olympic Games from Berlin, it seemed that Germany was regaining a degree of self-respect and reputation lost after the humiliations of the First World War, but radio and press reports were already carefully controlled by Propaganda Minister Goebbels. The government actively promoted the manufacture and distribution of the *Volksempfänger* (people's receiver), a moderately priced radio now in millions of homes and an essential tool in the dissemination of propaganda and information.

Berta had often lamented her isolated existence on the estate, with only books for company. She avidly read travel books which Emil borrowed from the public library in Aachen. Now, as well as being informed about political developments, she enjoyed popular music and classical concerts. The radio was indispensable in promoting the concept of *Volksgemeinschaft* – a community of the people. The German population was to be spiritually united across class divides in a sense of common racial identity and national purpose.

Minny's training involved learning about the supply and sale of pharmaceutical ingredients. Apprentices were taken to dimly-lit warehouses storing huge sacks of raw materials releasing exotic scents from all over the world. For part of the week she attended the *Höhere Handelsschule* (School of Commerce), and was taught bookkeeping, filing, office procedure, typing and shorthand.

With fellow trainees she watched the *Karneval* processions, which in the mid-1930s represented one of the few occasions when political comment and satire could be expressed. In 1937, after Abyssinia, the northern part of present-day Ethiopia, had been annexed by Mussolini's Italian government, the procession included a caricature of Haile Selassie, its head of state. Even Goebbels appeared one year, his characteristic angular features moulded in exaggerated garish colours.

Finally, in the spring of 1938 Berta yielded to pleas for a *Karneval* costume, and the visiting seamstress sewed Minny a traditional Dirndl dress. 1938 would be the final year the celebrations were staged until after the war, and the first and last time she would have a costume, consisting of a dress with black velvet-laced bodice over a white blouse with puffed sleeves. The full black skirt, decorated with tiny coloured flowers, was covered with a green apron. She still has the apron. A Tyrolean hat decorated with feather and white crocheted socks with black patent shoes completed the outfit. But in the month of her eighteenth birthday, her mother still chaperoned her at the *Karneval* ball, held in the Quellenhof, Aachen's most prestigious and expensive hotel, where wealthy guests bathed in baths fed by steaming medicinal waters to ease ailments, and townspeople used public pools for a small charge. Weeks later, Hitler annexed Austria – the *Anschluss* – and troops received a rapturous welcome.

Vienna 15th March 1938 after Anschluss

Herr Nellessen was a generous employer. Of a similar build to Emil – they were both of medium height and weight – he passed on good quality unwanted suits and coats. In the summer of 1938 he presented Emil with a gold pocket watch engraved with a dedication commemorating 25 years of "faithful service" since 1913, encompassing four years of absence during the First World War.

But his generosity extended further. While Emil had travelled widely in Europe as the Nellessen chauffeur, he had never taken a holiday with his own family. His own annual summer holiday over, Herr Nellessen withdrew to his wife's

Dutch estate and offered Emil the use of his car for travels around Germany over three weeks in the autumn of 1938.

They had no inkling that they would never again take a holiday together, or that many of the towns and cities visited would soon be destroyed by war. Herr Nellessen, though, may have sensed the urgency and pressed them to take the offer before it was too late.

To be able to take a holiday was a privilege envied by Minny's fellow apprentices. Only reluctantly did Herr Geilenkirchen, whom she had to approach personally, allow absence from training, since apprentices were an essential element of the workforce. Sleeping in guest houses and hotels and eating in restaurants were new experiences. Conscious of limited funds, they also stayed with aunts and uncles, whose households were scattered around central and southern Germany.

Emil had five sisters. Tante Gretchen and Tante Fanny's Heidelberg apartment was filled with massive, dark, heavy pieces of furniture. Cousin Willi, who ran a car showroom, put them up in Karlsruhe. Minny and Erhard had little input into the route or places visited, as Berta and Emil planned the journey without reference to their children's preferences; at eighteen Minny was expected to follow her parents' wishes. But Emil was eager to expand his family's knowledge of both personal and German history. At Eschelbach near Heidelberg, where he had attended school and lived as a child, he searched in a small secluded churchyard for the names of his father and other Rössler ancestors carved on crumbling weather-beaten tombstones. They listened dutifully to explanations of networks of relationships, complicated by the fact that his mother was his father's second wife.

Genealogical research flourished in the Third Reich, as potential employees in many public spheres were required to produce proof of Aryan ancestry – the *Ahnenpass* (ancestry passport) – composed of multiple documents establishing "pure" ancestry. Minny has no memory of having to prove suitability in this way, but her ancestry would have been checked before she was accepted for her apprenticeship. Emil was fiercely patriotic and his interest was primarily fuelled by pride in family history.

A family *Ahnenpass* survives which was issued for one of Minny's cousins, the daughter of Emil's eldest sister Susanne, showing details of Rössler grandparents, great-grandparents and great-great-grandparents, whose names were recorded on the Eschelbach gravestones.

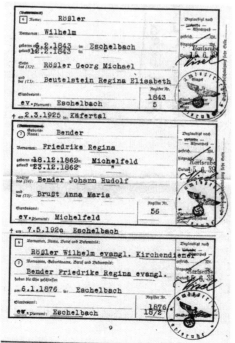

Extract from Rössler Ahnenpass ('Ancestry Passport')

If only Minny had paid more attention. In the southern German state of Baden-Württemberg, at Schloss Hohenlohe-Langenburg, which admitted visitors to parts of the castle and was the family seat of Graf Hohenlohe-Langenburg, Emil searched out and located a yellowed pane of glass in a leaded window of an outhouse, where he had scratched his initials E.R. while in the services of the Count, his first job after completing an apprenticeship. In one surviving photograph from this trip taken by Minny, her family are standing by the car – a "Wanderer" model – dressed in coats, although it was only September.

Family Holiday 1938

They travelled with the top pulled back, in goggles and headscarves, luggage strapped to a rack at the rear. By late September they reached the Bodensee, known as Lake Constance in English, where in Friedrichshafen the main attraction was the recently opened Zeppelin Museum. In a huge exhibition hall the *Graf Hindenburg* had been reconstructed for visitors. From a staircase positioned under the machine, Minny peered into the passenger cabin slung beneath the fated airship, which had exploded in 1937, and realised that in ignorance she had imagined passengers travelling in the ship itself rather than in a separate compartment.

Pleasure in new places and experiences during those weeks contrasted with the tense and uncertain atmosphere of the political situation. Nazi banners and flags fluttered from buildings, troops paraded in the streets. The Munich agreement between Hitler and Chamberlain was signed just before they returned home. German soldiers marched into the Sudetenland – an area of Czechoslovakia with a German-speaking population – and were enthusiastically welcomed. War seemed to be averted for the time being, and jokes about Chamberlain circulated. Berta and Emil could not pronounce his name.

Tante Lydia and Onkel Philip, with a grandchild

At Tante Lydia's house in Neckarsteinach near Heidelberg, the personal and the political collided. Tante Lydia, one of Emil's elder sisters, ran a small guest house (full board 3 Reichsmark!) perched on a small hill overlooking the river Neckar. Minny revelled in a household where people were constantly coming and going, unlike their own quiet, secluded existence. Onkel Philip oversaw the dyeing of fabrics and leather in a local factory, and when sirens sounded at midday he walked home for lunch shared with the paying guests.

Before marriage to Philip Eichler in the 1920s, Lydia had worked as a midwife and nursing sister and befriended an unmarried Jewish girl on her ward, who gave birth to a girl fathered by an Aryan. Tante Lydia adopted the child and raised her along with her own child, Minny's cousin Heinz. Her adopted daughter Hilde Eichler, being only half-Jewish, was as yet not affected by the full indignities and exclusions forced on Jewish citizens, which had progressively been passed from 1933 onwards, of which the Nuremberg laws of 1935 were the most restrictive to date.

During that visit in 1938 Minny witnessed discussions between Hilde, her birth mother and her adoptive mother as to how to circumvent the laws. Hilde, confident that her Aryan name and certificate of baptism offered relative protection for the time being, feared for her mother, who was in greater danger through bearing a Jewish name. Much later Minny learned that Hilde was successful in reaching Seattle where she married and raised a family, but her mother lost her life at sea *en route* to Canada.

Soon after they returned from their travels, the Synagogue in Aachen was burnt down on the night of 8th/9th November, later known as *Kristallnacht*. Countrywide, synagogues and Jewish properties were targeted in a wave of organised attacks. Aachen had a moderately sized Jewish population. Minny could not fail to notice when townspeople were exhorted by signs in shop windows not to buy goods from Jewish shops. She did not heed these signs, but neither did she take the ominous happenings seriously or give them much thought. She admits she did not understand the political situation in enough depth to assess whether Nazi propaganda, which held Germany's Jewish population responsible for all society's ills, was actually credible.

Germans defend yourselves, do not buy from Jews, 1933

On the streets of Aachen, Nazi newspapers such as *Völkischer Beobachter* and *Der Stürmer* with inflammatory anti-Jewish headlines were set up in freestanding glass display stands for those who could not afford to buy papers. In 1935 a register of Jewish residents had been compiled in Aachen, recording a number of 1,276. But it is assumed that the number was actually higher, as many were not registered.

Nazi newspaper masthead

At Kaisersruh they were caught between two poles of opinion. On the one hand Herr Nellessen privately expressed disdain for and mistrust of the Nazi Party, but as one of the wealthiest landowners around Aachen he could not avoid being approached and pressurised by party officials for donations, with which he complied. With his knowledge, one of the house cooks used to slip away with food to a household she had formerly worked in, which sheltered several Jewish families. By contrast, Onkel Adolf, Berta's brother, became an enthusiastic Nazi supporter and strutted around in his brown party uniform, maintaining it was good for his business, an inn in the suburb of Vaalserquartier, on the border with Holland, which he ran with Berta's sister, Minny's namesake and godmother. In earlier years they had been landlords of the oldest inn in Cologne.

Even with the rise of National Socialism, Minny and her family continued to attend the Protestant church (Christuskirche) in the Richardstrasse. Party members were "encouraged" to leave the church and many outspoken clergy in Aachen from both Catholic and Protestant communities suffered imprisonment, fines and harassment in varying degrees for voicing opposition. The policy of *Gleichschaltung* – the gradual political "bringing into line" of all spheres of cultural and social life – was tightening its grip. As political decisions increasingly began to impact their lives, details of countless new edicts were followed on the Blaupunkt radio receiver.

The impending war made clear that her aspiration to become a dispensing chemist should be put on hold. "Look for a job," urged her parents, believing it would be preferable to build on the administrative and secretarial skills learned at the *Handelsschule*. At the *Arbeitsamt* (Job Centre) she learned of two possible secretarial openings, one with the Gestapo and one at the main Police Headquarters in Aachen, the *Polizeipräsidium*. After an interview and entrance exam at the police station, she was offered the job. With war on the horizon, employment of any sort was welcome and it was expected that the bulk of her salary be given to her parents. She admits today that she did not give any thought to the organisation she was joining, or the nature of the state she would now be working for. The overriding family concern was to be in work and earning a wage.

The Nazi government took over the traditional and rather conservative police force of the Weimar republic, gradually bringing its functions and roles into line, with Himmler appointed in overall charge from 1936 onwards. Many career policemen initially welcomed the regime, as it promised to uphold traditional German values and champion law and order. In some ways the Nazis made policing roles easier; the force was centralised and better equipped to combat crime, staffing was increased and equipment was modernised. Initially crime levels dropped. But at a price. The force was gradually transformed into an instrument of repression and eventually genocide.

Poster 1938, "The Police, your Friend and Helper"

The regime ensured that only loyal party members were given key administrative positions. The recently arrived police chief was a fanatical supporter, with a fearsome temper, who had risen swiftly through the ranks of the party, and who, it later emerged, had led the attack on the synagogue. He barked out orders, expected meticulous punctuality; others instinctively avoided him, knowing not to incur his displeasure. With very little idea of daily administrative procedures, he had been appointed after a career in industry because of his party loyalty, which was common practice. Junior employees were expected to show allegiance with the customary Hitler greeting and took an oath not to disclose information learned in the course of work.

By now she and her family knew they lived under a repressive and ruthless regime which did not tolerate opposition. At work a kind of unspoken understanding of their position hung in the air. Careless or flippant remarks were only exchanged with those one trusted. To colleagues making inadvisable comments the phrase *"dich kassieren sie ein"* was common – "they'll get you". The Gestapo was housed in a separate building. In all major towns, the *Polizeipräsidium*, where Minny worked, encompassed the *Verwaltungspolizei, Schutzpolizei* and *Kriminalpolizei*. The *Kriminalpolizei* dealt with public order, such as general law and order during bombings. The *Schutzpolizei* was responsible for matters like traffic violations, and the *Verwaltungspolizei* administered issues of public health, registration of addresses, passports, and certifications such as hunting licences.

Minny worked in the personnel department of the *Verwaltungspolizei*, dealing with administration and paperwork relating to employees, for instance notification of postings, insurance and training and career matters. Each local police station referred their paperwork to a central station. Every morning she distributed the post, took down the content of letters in shorthand and typed them, wearing oversleeves for protection against typewriter ink. On Saturday mornings the local prostitutes had to present themselves to be examined by a police doctor. After they were given a clean bill of health, her department stamped their licences for the coming week.

In the summer months of 1939, preparations for war were conspicuously evident. Since the previous year the *Westwall*, (also known as the Siegfried Line) a massive line of fortifications stretching for over 400 kilometres from just north of Aachen to the Swiss border, had been under construction. The government maintained it was primarily defensive, to deter French aggression on the Western Front. Thousands of labourers drafted into the *Organisation Todt,* named after the engineer in charge of the construction, had to be housed in civilian households while erecting barbed wire defences, bunkers and the characteristic triangular shaped concrete blocks that stood in deep snaking rows through the countryside, to prevent enemy tanks from crossing on to German soil.

Westwall anti-tank obstacles

Hitler and Himmler visited the region in April 1939 to inspect the completion of the work. Swathes of land around the city became out of bounds to civilians. Minny's parents grumbled as a section of their vegetable plot, plum trees, and part of the Nellessens' garden had to make way for a massive *Westwall* bunker, but this was partly compensated by extra funds brought in by an engineer who was billeted in their house; one evening around the kitchen table he explained with the aid of paper and pencil the strategic importance of the defences for Germany. The door of the bunker, constructed of concrete reinforced with steel, was so heavy that two men were needed to open it. At around the same time, the Nellessens' cellar was strengthened with additional beams and struts, as an extra bomb shelter, and a second bunker was erected for the adjacent farmhouse, owned by the Zintzen family. These custom-built bunkers consisted of several rooms, and were equipped with limited electricity, bunk beds with wooden slats, and benches.

But not only people had to be protected. In August, priceless medieval artefacts, jewelled reliquaries and illuminated manuscripts, many from the era of Charlemagne and his court, were removed from displays in the cathedral treasury and stored in safer surroundings, some being later housed in one of the towers flanking the famous Carolingian octagonal chapel. The imperial city of Aachen, with its unique history, had a particular place in the ideology of National Socialism; Charlemagne had presided over the first "German Reich". Other museums and the city archives also moved documents and works of art to safer outlying buildings and depositories.

Minny started her new job at the beginning of the summer of 1939. Within a few weeks they were at war.

CHAPTER FOUR

September 1939 – December 1943: War

On 1st September 1939, German troops crossed the Polish border, Chamberlain issued his ultimatum to Hitler's government, and on 3rd September the British gathered around radio sets to listen to his statement.

Minny was standing at the bottom of the main staircase in the *Polizeipräsidium* in Aachen when someone shouted that Britain had declared war. *"Wir haben Krieg!"* The news echoed around the building. Today, Minny admits: "I did not really comprehend its significance – in my ignorance I even thought war might be rather exciting!" The population of Aachen had reacted with unabated enthusiasm at the outbreak of hostilities in 1914, with cheering in the streets and an upbeat feeling of defiance. Now a quite different mood prevailed. Black-out orders had been issued, ration cards distributed. For months, through a hot tense summer, they had witnessed preparations, interpreted signs, but still hoping the seemingly inevitable might be avoided.

Maybe she never really believed it would happen. After all, earlier in the year she had paid 90 Reichsmark in advance for a trip to Berlin in September 1939 through the organisation *Kraft durch Freude* (strength through joy) – a National Socialist innovation promoting mass tourism and leisure activities – and was anticipating admiring sights and landmarks illustrated in schoolbooks: the *Siegessäule* – victory column – the four-horsed *Quadriga* chariot on the Brandenburg Gate. But her parents' generation had witnessed the First World War; their memories were still vivid. Minny was perplexed by Emil and Berta's reaction of fear and horror. Having rebuilt their lives after 1918, they now stood on the edge of yet another catastrophe. Minny could not imagine what war would mean in concrete terms for either family or country. She neither considered the rights or wrongs of the situation, nor had any clear notion of the "enemy" or why war had been declared. The basic English learned at school had only provided a hazy concept of the British, their empire or reasons for entering the war. Nor did the immediate trigger for the declaration of war – the invasion of Poland – have much resonance in her immediate experience. For anyone living on the western flank of Germany, Poland seemed as remote as London.

At Kaisersruh, the progress of hostilities was followed on the radio. From the declaration of war to the final capitulation of 1945, radio bulletins on the military situation – the *Wehrmachtsberichte* (army reports) – were broadcast daily, reporting on both war and home fronts, a unifying tool of national propaganda. Emil and Berta were thankful their son was too young to have been called up. The only words of English they ever learned related to conflict and battle.

In the weeks following the invasion of Poland, Polish prisoners-of-war began to arrive in Aachen and were housed in camps on the Krefelderstrasse, the main road Minny cycled along from Kaisersruh to work in the city. After her parents became fearful for her safety, as prisoners often escaped, a colleague offered to fetch her in his car. Even though she was almost twenty, her father still escorted her home after an evening out, and she resorted to carrying an umbrella for defence against potential assault. Polish prisoners were drafted in to work on the farms in the area, including those adjacent to the Kaisersruh estate, and in the coal mines around Würselen. But generally it seemed a phoney war, a situation which mirrored that in Britain; in Germany it was known as the *Sitzkrieg* – the sitting war.

The expected invasion from France, the perceived reasoning behind the *Westwall*, never materialised, constituting a major miscalculation on the part of Hitler. Official contingency plans, drawn up for the eventual evacuation of civilians, were never implemented. Many who had left the city, when war was declared, decided to return. Air raids and bombings had not yet started: the first Christmas of the war proved not to be significantly different in material terms from previous years.

Minny had always regarded the isolation of her home in the countryside as disadvantageous, but in the early stages of the war it ensured a better and more secure supply of food than for city dwellers. Those in the country might supplement allotted rations with locally available meat and dairy products from nearby farms, where farmers and workers essential to the war effort were exempt from being drafted into the *Wehrmacht*.

As the war progressed and rations were reduced, bartering illegally for food became essential. The government was intent at all costs on avoiding the widespread undernourishment and malnutrition experienced at the end of the First World War in 1918. Adequate food supply became a tool in maintaining morale. Soon after the start of the war, Berta and Emil bought a pig, installed him in the disused pigsty and mourned his passing when he was slaughtered and processed by the butcher from Würselen. The sausages, strung up in the laundry, were stolen one night by the pet dachshund for a litter of pups waiting in the stables.

Berta's enthusiastic peace-time bottling of garden produce guaranteed a more varied diet than that of her own mother, who had recently moved to live in the centre of Aachen with her younger daughter, Tante Minny, after the death of the latter's husband. Grandmother von Knappen never made a secret of her favouritism for her second daughter.

Throughout the war, before reporting for work, Minny Rössler dutifully and with growing resentment delivered heavy bags of surplus vegetables and jams to her aunt's apartment, and food to share at work, balancing everything on her bicycle. As train, tram and bus services became more unpredictable, she learned to rely on two feet or two wheels.

New words entered the vocabulary. *Hamstern* meant collecting and storing foodstuffs, many acquired by bartering in the black market that quickly established itself. Much of Minny's *hamstern* was done by bicycle, riding along rural tracks between farms and cottages, swapping and acquiring food and other commodities, such as mutton and wool from a family friend who was a shepherd. Coffee was replaced by *Muckefuck* – ersatz coffee made from malt.

In the spring of 1940, to celebrate the Führer's birthday in April, the city authorities organised collections of iron and metalwork for smelting to help the armaments industry. Aachen street corners and squares lost statues that embodied city history and folklore. A statue of Charlemagne on the fountain in the market place fell victim to the purge, as did ancient church bells. Railings disappeared from city parks and the wrought iron gates at the entrance to the Nellessen estate were removed.

Apprehensive as to how hostilities would develop, they witnessed what would be referred to as *Die erste deutsche*

Besatzung or *Einquartierung* – the first German "occupation" or billeting. Soldiers waiting for the planned invasion of Belgium, Holland and Luxembourg, known as *Fall Gelb* (Case Yellow), many from Schleswig Holstein and the northern areas of Germany, were billeted with civilians - over 40,000 in the whole city. Officers occupied rooms in the large estate house at Kaisersruh, while the infantry soldiers slept on straw mattresses in the outhouses and horses lived in the stables. In the yard stood their carts, piled up with provisions of flour and pulses in huge sacks.

One soldier, a baker by trade, helped Berta bake loaves to feed everyone. In the cold winter of 1939, as thick snow lay on the ground, they sat around the kitchen table in the evenings, sharing rations of rum, and singing to the accompaniment of harmonicas. Minny could not help gaining the impression that if this was war, then it was fun and convivial.

In the following May they were ordered to advance. Within a few weeks, Germany had conquered Belgium, the Netherlands and France. Minny stood in the yard, helped load belongings onto carts, and watched as they harnessed their horses and waved goodbye, eager to be seeing action after months of anticipation and uncertainty. She was given mementoes and even a promise of marriage.

Within a few weeks they received word that not one had survived the first onslaughts. Most had left behind a record of their addresses, anticipating the worst but not really believing it. Minny and Emil packed up watches, photos and keepsakes – sent back to them by the soldiers' commanding officers – to post back to families in Schleswig Holstein and Hamburg. This first experience of the reality of war shook her. She had shared the men's lives for months. Now they were dead. Their families even wrote letters of thanks for returned belongings.

Not until May 1940 did British military aircraft fly over Aachen. On 12ᵗʰ May the first bombs fell and the first casualties were recorded. As war progressed, the intensity and frequency of attacks increased. The British later expressly declared that one of their aims was to weaken the morale of civilians by bombing urban areas, towns and cities with no strategic military importance. Minny kept a small brown leather suitcase, containing clothes, shoes, documents, savings books and jewellery in the hallway by the front door in readiness for sirens sounding in Haaren or Würselen.

On leaving the house, they snatched small torches, whose switches had to be constantly clicked on, and hastily used the toilet before leaving, as there was no sanitation in the bunker. Berta had previously hauled extra bedding – feather duvets, mattresses and blankets – into the shelter, for when the sirens sounded at night. Hammocks could be slung for extra occupants.

Prisoners-of-war forced into labour on nearby farms also took shelter when the sirens started, although according to regulations they were supposed to occupy a separate section of the bunker. If there was an air raid while Minny was at work in the city, everyone filed down to the cellars, which had been strengthened and equipped for sheltering employees.

It was safer to be caught during an air raid in a purpose-built shelter than in reinforced cellars, which might collapse, suffocating and burying alive those trapped inside, while shelters withstood hits and were virtually indestructible. After the war not even explosives could destroy them. Remains can still be located in Aachen today.

At the *Polizeipräsidium*, a state of war meant additional and specific duties. With others, Minny was trained in *Luftschutz* – air raid protection. She was issued with a gas mask and boiler suit, learned how to operate fire equipment and earned a certificate of competence after an exam taken in the grounds of the Quellenhof Hotel, where the ornamental fountains and ponds were put to wartime use to supply hosepipes with water for extinguishing blazes.

Poster celebrating Day of the German Police 1941

Working at the police station for the state also brought privileges. The *Reichsarbeitsdienst* (Reich labour force) had been introduced by the NSDAP in 1935, to engage all young men in useful employment in the service of the state, thereby reducing unemployment. Since 1939, all young women between the ages of 18 and 25 also had to serve 6 months in domestic work, agriculture and community projects, but with the increasing shortage of men as the war progressed, many were put to work in munitions and other industries. From 1941 onwards, it was extended and became known as the *Kriegshilfsdienst* (war labour force). Minny was exempt. Tension surfaced in the Third Reich between the perceived calling of women as mothers and homemakers, and an increasing need for women to fill jobs essential for the war effort, especially after men were called up and fell in their thousands.

In the spring of 1940 Minny is recorded as having joined the National Socialist Party. Her records in the NSDAP register note that membership was applied for in May of 1940, acceptance was granted on 1st July and that a membership card was issued in July 1941. She is registered in the Köln/Aachen *Gau* – a term denoting the administrative districts formed by the National Socialist regime – but does not recollect signing an application or the issue of a membership card, explaining that "Everyone was automatically signed up – we had no choice". Viewed in the context of her employment at the police station and membership of the BDM, it is likely that employees were "invited" to join, with membership a condition of continuing employment. Over sixty years later, debate in the German press reflects a similar assertion, in which prominent German writers, found to be members, have also claimed automatic membership occurred without their knowledge. This is disputed by some historians (see Historical Note 2).

At home Minny often ignored the air-raid sirens, trusting in the relative safety of the countryside. If they sounded at night, she even stayed in bed. During the first bombing raids of 1940 they joined the Nellessens in their cellar, rather than going to the bunker. But as air attacks increased, the windows of the grand old house were shattered and it suffered damage. In the summer of 1940, the Nellessen family moved to the Quellenhof, where Minny started delivering their post. Soon they left for Holland, leaving Emil in charge to secure Kaisersruh and oversee the estate in their absence. Heavy antique furniture was draped in sheets and eventually put into storage, along with huge Oriental carpets, custom-woven to fit the rooms, and delicate silk fabrics that had hung at windows and on walls. On the first floor, in elegant shuttered reception rooms, glass cases displayed delicate porcelain, watches and clocks. The collections were carried down to the cellar, wrapped in cloths and blankets, and sealed in behind a cellar wall. The Nellessen family never returned to live in the house. At the start of the war, Emil, born in 1887 and too old for active service, was not called up. In addition to administering Kaisersruh, he was tasked with overseeing Georg Nellessen's second family estate, Gut Schönthal, a brief cycle ride away and likewise deserted by its occupants, Herr Nellessen's wider family members.

After the departure of the first billeted units, in the closing months of 1940 a second German "occupation" or billeting took place, referred to as *die zweite deutsche Besatzung* in the privacy of the family. A non-combat intelligence unit, mainly consisting of officers, occupied the recently vacated house. Many came from southern Germany and Berlin. Minny experienced the brash, forthright, somewhat arrogant ways of Berliners. At the time she did not know or even care to consider the reasons for their presence, or what they were anticipating. Of more immediate concern was the enjoyment of their company and living for the moment.

"He's too old for you", remarked her mother, observing how one officer, Hans, a widower from Munich with an adult son, was obviously drawn to Minny. When the unit was posted to France, Minny received letters from Hans through the *Feldpost* (military post), but the unit's exact location remained secret, the address merely consisting of a coded number. Arrival of post marked a highlight in everyone's day, as news, even of casualties, was welcome. Minny eagerly ran to intercept the postman, sparing him a walk up the drive from the main road. Parcels of French perfume and sandals with cork platform heels arrived. Hans was then posted to Russia and began to send small square packets of pungent Russian tea. It was common practice for *Wehrmacht* soldiers and officers to send home items from locations occupied by German forces, and to take goods back, when on home leave. The conquered territories supplied a large proportion of foodstuffs for the German population at home, at the expense of their indigenous populations, where millions suffered malnutrition and starvation, but as the war progressed and territories were re-conquered by the Allies, especially in the east, rationing in Germany by necessity became more stringent.

Hans was later reported missing in the battle for Stalingrad. The precise timing of the "second" billeting of soldiers, and their function at Kaisersruh, is unclear. The sequence of Hans' postings suggest he was stationed at Kaisersruh in the late summer and early autumn of 1940. The unit may have been positioned in Aachen in preparation for the planned invasion of Britain, Operation *Seelöwe* (Sealion), which was postponed after British air superiority became evident and eventually cancelled in September 1940. They might also have been destined for France from the outset, moving there in late 1940, or even early 1941. Hans' military record, which could have shed light on these issues, can no longer be traced.

In March 1941, records state that Emil applied for Party membership and was accepted in April. It is not clear why, at this relatively late stage, he took such a step. Was he pressurised by officers of the Intelligence Unit billeted at Kaisersruh? They would have noted that although he had not been called up to serve in the *Wehrmacht*, as his age group were not yet conscripted, he had light duties looking after the Nellessen's estates in their absence.

When in June 1941 Hitler launched Operation Barbarossa – the invasion of Russia – ignoring the non-aggression treaty signed with Stalin two years previously on 23rd August 1939, Minny's boss was posted to Minsk in present-day Belarus, a part of Soviet territory invaded and occupied by German forces, and expressed preferences as to which members of staff he wished to accompany him. To her horror he let it be known this included her. A delicate and dangerous situation now needed to be handled carefully. A trusted doctor was approached and provided medical certification that her appendix needed removing immediately. Although he was in police employment, he at once recognised her predicament. In a makeshift operating theatre set up in a cellar, she underwent an operation by flickering light during an air raid, and evaded transferal to Minsk. The secretary who went in her place never returned.

July 1941 witnessed the first large scale bombing of the city of Aachen. As the Russian campaign progressed, and America entered the war at the end of 1941, the German people were continuously urged not to lose heart. But life was conducted in a permanent state of fear for oneself and for family members, fear of denunciation, fear for the nation, fear of what might follow "afterwards". *"Geniesse den Krieg, der Friede wird schrecklich sein"* ran a popular saying – "enjoy the war, peace will be terrible".

The cathedral, symbol of the city and of national patriotic pride, was particularly vulnerable to attack. From the summer of 1941, teams of young people had been trained to keep watch during air raids and extinguish fires, continuing their voluntary duty until late in 1944. The cathedral suffered many hits and several areas caught fire or were damaged, but the basic structure survived. The Rössler family attempted a semblance of normal life and went out to eat at a restaurant in Aachen in

1941, ordering Belgian mussels, a regional speciality still inexplicably available. As they returned home through darkened city streets and left the tram in Haaren to walk back to Kaisersruh, an air attack on Aachen began. They took cover on the edge of the cemetery and watched as the silhouette of the cathedral was dramatically illuminated against the evening sky, lit by fires caused by waves of incendiary bombs dropped by British planes.

After the most devastating attacks, when areas of the city were reduced to rubble and Minny was unable to get to work, she rode her bicycle to an outpost on the Krefelderstrasse, where radio equipment (*Funkanlagen*) was housed and from where a colleague might offer a ride by four-wheel-drive or in a motorcycle sidecar, negotiating devastated streets and weaving around the piles of smoking and unstable ruins of bombed and collapsed buildings. City-dwellers whose homes were destroyed or damaged in air raids were entitled to receive meals from temporary kitchens set up in different city districts. At the police headquarters she helped distribute food cooked in the basement and carried up in huge steaming containers. Colleagues whose apartments had become uninhabitable took to sleeping in their offices and appeared at lunch-time with plates, bowls and cutlery to receive a nourishing hot meal of soup or stew, mopped up with *Kommissbro*t, loaves of robust rye bread, which was also standard ration for soldiers in the field.

Minny was required to stand on the street for the *Winterhilfswerk* (Winter Aid Organisation), the "charitable" arm of the Nazi Party, rattling a tin can and selling limited editions of tiny painted metal figures of policemen dressed in different uniforms and performing civil functions. The proceeds were used to relieve hardship after air raids, and to provide food and clothing for townspeople during the colder winter months.

The charity was one more tool in fostering a sense of civic solidarity - through donations everyone contributed to a common cause, especially vital in times of hardship and war.

Postage stamp issued to support Nazi charity

In 1942 Emil was approached by an acquaintance who ran a hardware business in the city. Herr Kreuz's daughter Anita had completed her compulsory service in the labour force, and was already working as a secretary in a police station in the Mauerstrasse. "Could she", he asked, "be introduced through Minny to her superiors at the police headquarters?"

After an interview, Anita was found a job in the radio and communications section, located in the cellar, where she learned to signal in Morse. They addressed each other as "Fraulein Rössler" and "Fraulein Kreuz", although their families were acquainted. Anita kept a diary right through the war. It was safer to record feelings and thoughts on paper, rather than risk an ill-advised remark. If rumours or stories of atrocities were whispered amongst colleagues, others would quickly urge silence. In the charged climate of propaganda, rumour and counter-rumour, each person chose what or whom to believe. Pieces of news contrary to the official party line might be repeated at home to trusted family members, but could go no further.

Minny at Kaisersruh 1942

In the relative safety of home, Minny sat at the radio, trying to pick up news in German from abroad to form a clearer picture of events. Emil disapproved. He repeated the party line. *"Diesen Krieg"* he said, *"werden wir gewinnen"* – "we'll win this war". He was comparing his hopes for victory with the defeat of the last war, but he also knew that disloyalty carried the death penalty.

When Minny witnessed groups of Jews with yellow stars sewn onto their clothing being forced into trucks at a city crossroads, the official explanation was *"Die Juden werden in Sicherheit gebracht"* – the Jews are being taken to a place of safety. At work she was urged not to enquire further. Many had already left by whatever means possible, but those who remained were destined for deportation. In 1940 it is estimated that approximately 800 Jewish citizens still lived in Aachen. From April 1941, several Jewish "safe houses" were established, where families were forced together into cramped quarters. Between 1942 and 1944 deportations from the entire Rhineland, including Aachen, were conducted, destined for Theresienstadt, Auschwitz and other camps in the East. Fear for one's life prevented questioning what was happening. When Emil heard, through the grapevine, that a group was scheduled to leave, he tried to make contact with a Jewish colleague from the First World War, but it was already too late. The excuse offered by so many after the war – *"Davon haben wir nichts gewusst"* – "we didn't know about any of that" – is no longer credible. As the war progressed, evidence for the fate of Jewish citizens mounted daily as rumours circulated and eye-witness reports increased, but suspicions were not openly voiced or acted upon through fear. As the balance of the war shifted in favour of the Allies, comments even circulated that Germany's defeats were retribution for the fate of the Jews.

In spite of government attempts to suppress the reality of the extent of German losses in the Russian campaign towards late 1942, snippets of information filtered through. Soldiers fighting in Russia came home on leave and told of the horrors and the hopelessness of the campaign. A neighbour's son, Peter, was one of those who had a brief respite from the front. Pegging out washing on a warm summer day in 1942, Minny exchanged a few words with him before he left. "I don't think I'll ever come home," he said. He was correct in his premonition. In newsreels at cinemas, images of victorious soldiers being welcomed by indigenous populations and territorial gains continued to be shown, but Stalingrad marked a change in the public mood. The senseless slaughter could no longer be covered up.

Simultaneously, anti-British propaganda had become more explicit. A 1941 publication *Raubstaat England* (Robber state England) documented British history in graphic detail, focusing on the brutalities of colonial rule throughout the eighteenth and nineteenth centuries. Colour and black and white photos had to be bought separately and pasted in to an album, to form a complete picture of the insidious British character.

Propaganda

But hardships were relieved by respites when a birthday was celebrated, someone returned from the front, or it simply felt good to be alive. At cinemas, Zara Leander films provided mental escape from everyday realities, always preceded by rousing newsreels of triumphant German troops in action.

Minny 1943

Being confined in bunkers during air raids fostered shared comradeship as songs were sung and stories exchanged. One night at Kaisersruh in the summer of 1943 the air raid sirens sounded. As Minny responded to her father's continued shouts to leave the bedroom, part of the wall collapsed and a heavy painting crashed to the floor where the bed stood.

The house had not sustained a direct hit, but a bomb had exploded directly adjacent to the garage. Surrounded by piles of glass from shattered windows, the worst damage inflicted so far, Emil impressed on his family the relative value of houses and possessions, compared with people's lives. They remained unconvinced.

Bomb-damaged Rössler home

The next day Soviet prisoners-of-war from the Ukraine, supervised by German soldiers, were sent to help with clearing rubble. Housed in camps, they had previously been registered at the *Polizeipräsidium,* the women dressed in heavy padded jackets and headscarves. One soldier unearthed family photographs buried amongst the debris and handed them to Berta in a gesture of kindness. Maybe he remembered his own family at home. With building materials obtained from Würselen, the prisoners turned their hand to re-glazing broken windows, re-plastering and painting walls, and replacing dislodged roof tiles.

In the attic under the roof, the trunk and other stored items had escaped damage, but the kitchen was unusable. Observing the predicament, the prisoners, used to living off the land, demonstrated how to cook steaming vegetable stews, with turnips, cabbages and potatoes, over open fires in the yard, in huge zinc vats that were normally used to transport washing.

Friendly and generous, they shared their skills by gestures and sign language. They could have tried to escape, but conditions at Kaisersruh, difficult as they were, were preferable to the harsh existence they experienced in the camps where they were housed, not to mention the improved rations. They were skilled in the art of air-drying fruit, stringing slices of cored apples and pears in neat rows on lines suspended in the outhouses and stables.

Replacements for crockery lost in air raids could be obtained in nearby Würselen using coupons issued for the purpose. As air-raids and bombing increased in frequency, Emil had buried silver and mementoes from the Middle East near the house in a zinc vat, which suffered a direct hit, as did the greenhouse. Treu the donkey, who lived in the stables, was killed by a bomb blast. Scavenging in the dirt, Minny uncovered a small silver fox, pitted and with one leg blown off, but otherwise unscathed. They threw silver spoons into the lake and loaded other silver items into a wheelbarrow, pushing it into the park as night fell. The contents were dug into the earth under a clump of rhododendron bushes at dusk, but Emil must have been observed, for when he attempted to retrieve them after hostilities ceased, nothing remained. Some heirlooms were saved, taken to Tante Lydia's house in Neckarsteinach, buried in the Nellessen's cellar, or sent by post to Tante Gretchen in Heidelberg and retrieved in 1945. The silver fox and items of silver cutlery survive to this day among Minny's possessions.

In February 1943, Soviet troops had regained control of Stalingrad and Leningrad, with colossal casualties on both sides. Hitler ordered a "scorched earth" policy, instructing retreating German units to destroy everything in their path. In the first public admission by the German leadership that the tide was turning and the country faced unprecedented dangers, Goebbels delivered a speech in Berlin on 18th February, urging the population to prepare for "total war". The vehemence and frequency of exhortations to continue holding out at any cost, and to brace oneself for personal sacrifice, increased. The Allies prepared to advance through Italy; units were issued with booklets to review their knowledge of German uniforms.

In May the last German units in North Africa had capitulated. By the close of the year Allied and Axis powers had engaged in brutal fighting, as the Allies gained a foothold on Italian soil, and Allied leaders had met at Casablanca and Tehran to discuss a possible post-war order.

Tehran Conference 1943

As German cities continued to witness waves of sustained bombing, radio broadcasts still held out the promise of the *Endsieg* (final victory), exhorting the population not to succumb to a loss of morale.

By December no amount of propaganda could disguise the worsening situation. At Christmas, private travel to visit family was forbidden throughout the Reich. Emil followed the customary tradition of cutting down a fir tree in the woods, decorating it in secret and summoning the family with a small bell to view it on Christmas Eve. But roast goose and casseroled hare were not on the menu. The fifth Christmas and New Year at war were overshadowed by a feeling of foreboding.

CHAPTER FIVE

1944: Evacuation

At the turn of the year, German civilians are worn down by bombing, increasing privations and mounting setbacks. The unique geographical position of Aachen will lead, by the closing months of 1944, to the destruction, invasion and occupation of the city. Each family will be confronted with the agonising decision of whether to stay and hide out in a cellar, or to evacuate ahead of advancing enemy troops.

By January, the local *Wehrbezirkskommando*, the district military unit for the recruitment and call up of civilians, has moved into the empty main estate house at Kaisersruh, as their quarters in town have become uninhabitable after an air raid. They employ ex-soldiers who have become unfit for duty, and those from a variety of civilian occupations before the war.

The Allies are fighting their way up Italy. Hitler has moved Field Marshal Erwin Rommel – the "Desert Fox" defeated in the North Africa campaign – to Normandy to take command of the defences against an anticipated Allied invasion in the West. Rommel becomes a heroic figure in the minds of the population.

Erwin Rommel

Constant air raids leave nerves in a state of exhaustion. Many German cities are suffering a similar fate; experiences of terror under bombardment are shared by millions across the country. Cologne, Lübeck, Hamburg: the list of historic and cultural centres reduced to rubble seems never-ending, although the ancient university city of Heidelberg seems so far to have escaped serious damage. The parcels of keepsakes and family valuables sent to Tante Gretchen and Tante Fanny in Heidelberg are therefore safer than in Aachen. Minny's 24th birthday passes almost unnoticed. The annual *Karneval* celebrations before Lent are a mere memory. This year children will not scrabble in the streets for sweets raining down from *Karneval* floats or eat flat greasy potato pancakes – *Reibekuchen* – from paper cones at the *Kirmes* fair in Würselen. Food has become mere sustenance. Everyone forages for provisions and many pool their resources.

Minny has become good friends with Anita Kreuz, her colleague at the police station, with whom she is now on Christian name terms. Anita comes up to Kaisersruh for coffee, but cannot return the invitation. Her family home in the

THE BRIDE'S TRUNK · 95

Adalbertstrasse has been destroyed in the bombing raid of 14th July of the previous year, 1943, one of the most devastating raids so far, when large parts of the city centre burned for days, hundreds of civilians were killed, and many lost everything.

Anita describes a visit to the site of her home two weeks after the raid. Everything was so warm from the intense conflagration that she undressed to her underwear before descending the cellar steps. As she pushed the door open, large wicker baskets filled with washing were visible for a split second before crumbling to ash before her eyes. Crystal bowls placed there for safekeeping had melted to an undistinguishable mass, but some porcelain miraculously survived. The Kreuz family have moved to another apartment in the Brabantstrasse, furnished with donations from friends. Large areas of the city centre are no more than mounds of rubble, but townspeople still try to keep to a routine of going to work amongst the wreckage.

Tante Lydia in Neckarsteinach has become a central information point for coordinating the whereabouts of family members. Minny spends a few days' holiday with her and meets Anita, also on a short break, by accident on the street. Anita has been sleeping on a friend's sofa, so she moves in with Minny at Tante Lydia's for a few days.

In Aachen, the ferocity of aerial attacks by the Royal Air Force intensifies. On 11th April, Minny is on duty at work as the sirens sound. A major bombardment is underway. Everyone follows the drill and heads for the basement. Part of the building takes a direct hit in the early hours of the morning, over the cellar where five or six are sheltering, including Minny. After an initial dull impact, a deathly silence. They instinctively feel they cannot escape unaided, although walls and ceiling have not given way. They wait, with mounting fear and claustrophobia, not knowing what is happening outside and unable to help themselves as the door is jammed shut. Shouting is useless. After some hours, they hear scratching and knocking as rescuers burrow their way in, break through and lead them to street level through the smouldering remains of the wing where she was at work. It will remain unusable, but business will continue in other undamaged sections.

Bomb-damaged Police HQ, Aachen

One of Minny's colleagues who has helped in the rescue offers to drive her home, but as many areas of the city centre have suffered a similar fate to their workplace, an indirect route has to be found avoiding impassable streets of burning buildings and piles of unstable rubble. Clouds of dust and smoke hamper visibility. Delayed explosions are still going off and large areas of the city centre are burning. Minny's colleague, frantic for the safety of his wife and five children, first drives with her towards Vaalserquartier, a suburb on the

Dutch border, where they find his house totally destroyed. Clambering over the ruins he salvages a human arm which he recognizes as his wife's from the wedding ring still attached to the finger of her right hand. When Minny eventually reaches home, traumatised by the horror of what she has just witnessed, she learns that her father, Emil, has tried to reach the city by bicycle to search for her; he returns to find her safe.

When air raid sirens sound at Kaisersruh, the family slip through the hedge and join the Zintzen family in the bunker at the farm, as the shelter serving the main house now serves the *Wehrbezirkskommando*. Frau Schlösser, the wife of one of the unit employees, pushes a pram from the city every evening with three children. The Schlössers have a business in the city centre selling bed linen. They share the evening meal and bed down in rooms normally used by Minny, Berta and Emil. Minny and her family sleep in the main Kaisersruh house. Frau Schlösser feels safer spending the night in the country in case of a raid, and then pushes the children back to the city the following morning, a pattern to which many have resorted.

D-Day landings 6th June 1944

News of the Allied landings in France in June signal mixed feelings of trepidation and relief, as the end, whatever form it might take, can surely not now be far off.

Emil, aged 56, along with others in his age group, has been called up and is guarding Allied prisoners-of-war at Soest in Westphalia. He has hitherto been occupied as estates administrator in the Nellessens' absence, but the worsening situation necessitates new and desperate regulations which are constantly being announced and enforced. Men previously exempted from call-up due to age are now enlisted.

Emil in uniform, 1944

A plot to assassinate Hitler has failed, the perpetrators rounded up. Everyone fears even more repressive measures to quell opposition, although propaganda triumphantly asserts that he has survived to fulfill his destiny and lead the German people to victory. Few believe this anymore.

Erhard, now 15, has been sent to boarding school in Monschau, in the wooded and hilly Eifel area south of Aachen, as his school, the *Kaiser-Karls Gymnasium* (Emperor Charlemagne Grammar School), the oldest grammar school in the city, has suffered bomb damage. Minny now cycles to the station in Aachen every Sunday, her free day, and takes the train to visit him, carrying a basket filled with home produce to supplement rations. He and his companions are eagerly awaiting her arrival, and that of the spare cakes and sausage, at the railway station. They are even able to eat out in a restaurant with ration coupons. It becomes important for people to develop routines that, precarious as they are, enable them to keep going with a semblance of personal control over their lives.

After the breakout from the Normandy beachheads, the Allies' progress is followed on the radio. Canadian, British and American army groups are under the command of General Eisenhower, who envisages swift progress across the Rhine and on to Berlin by Christmas. The 21st Army Group, led by General Bernard Montgomery and comprising British and Canadian forces, is tasked with advances across northern France, Luxembourg, Belgium, the Netherlands and into Germany, in particular with securing ports. It is hard to imagine how the tide can turn again for the German nation, in spite of so-called *Wunderwaffen* (miracle weapons) emphasised by the propaganda machine. The first V1 rocket attack has recently been launched on London, but *Endsieg* (final victory) is a pipe dream.

The German government in increasing desperation now enlists boys born in 1928 who reach 16 in 1944. Minny's brother Erhard has reached this milestone at the beginning of August, but a few weeks previously he has volunteered, along with other eager teenagers, as a *Flakhelfer* (flak helper) trained in *Flak* (abbreviation for *Flugabwehrkanone* - anti-aircraft gun) defence techniques. In a state of excitement at finally being able to contribute to the war effort, he calls on Minny, on duty in the city, to pass on the news. In peacetime she had bathed him in a tin tub on the kitchen table, wheeled him around the estate in a wooden hand cart to forage for edible mushrooms, balanced him on bicycle handlebars for a ride to school in Würselen. Now she collects food and delivers it to him at military quarters in Vaalserquartier. Berta cooks him stewed strawberries with vanilla custard.

Erhard's first duty is as one of the teenagers manning anti-aircraft guns, at the Kronenberg, just below the *Pelzerturm* (Pelzer tower), on a strategic hill overlooking the city. He is responsible for adjusting the settings altering the elevation of the guns.

At the beginning of September there is little left to admire in the ancient and once beautiful city of Aachen. Over seventy large-scale air raids have been recorded, countless buildings have been destroyed or damaged, over two thousand civilians killed, and a similar number injured. Those still remaining are down to their last reserves. Many camp out in cellars or with relatives. Water and electricity are intermittent. Horror and tension grow as General Patton's American First Army is positioned not far from the borders of the Reich and has been ordered to take Aachen.

Contingency measures have theoretically been put in place for the defence of the Reich in the eventuality of enemy troops occupying German soil; as early as 13th July Hitler had issued appropriate orders on evacuation of civilians, and defined areas of responsibility for military and civilian authorities. But as Minny continues to report for work there is an overwhelming impression that no-one is in overall control and everyone must take responsibility for themselves as conflicting stories circulate. Should the unthinkable happen, who will direct operations? In principle, the military machine must be given priority in the defence of German territory, and evacuating civilians cannot be allowed to hamper troop movements. Numerous high ranking party officials have already fled.

To relieve tension, Anita and Minny walk in the Quellenhof park, where a brass band is playing to calm the atmosphere. The whole scene seems unreal. Their lives may soon end to musical accompaniment. They make casual, almost light-hearted remarks concerning which common acquaintances have lost houses or even lives.

Bomb-damaged Aachen railway station, mid-1944

Bands of wounded, exhausted and dishevelled soldiers are returning, many having walked hundreds of miles. Considering themselves released from their oaths, soldiers break down as they tell of what they have witnessed. Dozens are rounded up and hastily formed into units to help defend the *Westwall*, which as yet remains unbreached.

On 10th September, a clear, sunny, cool day, Heinrich Himmler visits Aachen and orders the population to continue holding out, emphasising its strategic importance for the regime. *"Aachen wird nicht geräumt,"* he assures the townspeople – "Aachen will not be evacuated". A general reaction of scepticism. Minny glimpses him on the street as she leans out of an office window. Divisions of the First US Army have reached Eupen, just a few kilometres away in Belgium.

On the following day, the 11th, a general order is issued to evacuate the remaining population. Local NSDAP head Eduard Schmeer, under orders from *Gau* district head Grohé, is to direct the evacuation. In theory, plans prepared down to the last detail are to be implemented with the precision of a military operation. But in practice widespread confusion and panic reign as loudspeakers boom out instructions on the street. Tanks, and vehicles carrying wounded and able-bodied soldiers clog the streets. Displaced and returning soldiers are directed to points where they can hastily be reconvened into new battalions, tasked with taking up positions for the defence of the city. They compete for access on the roads with those hurrying home to gather up belongings, snatch a hurried wash and food before being directed to the station, or setting off on foot.

Specific areas of Germany – parts of Thuringia, Westphalia, Silesia and Lower Saxony – are earmarked for thousands of civilians leaving Aachen. Some try to evade evacuation and hide out in cellars, but are driven out if discovered, and forced to leave. It is considered a treasonable offence to resist. After all, the order to evacuate came from the Führer himself.

At least Minny is still uninjured. The sick and wounded in hospitals cannot decide their fate and are at the mercy of others' decisions. Even now, there is looting as alcohol, food or household goods are plundered from damaged and abandoned homes, shops and warehouses. Those left in charge – the remaining higher party and military officials of the area – must implement final strategies and prepare to defend their city and the Westwall positions. The noise of enemy planes, *flak*, shots and distant artillery fire forms a constant backdrop. At the cathedral, groups of dedicated volunteers are still on fire duty. In the *Polizeipräsidium* there is conflicting advice as to how to act. Those not in positions of authority, such as Minny, are urged to get away while they are able. It is senseless continuing to report for work. What is it all for anyway? Minny returns to Kaisersruh, and remains there with her mother, as they try to reach a decision.

◆◆◆

On the evening of the 11ᵗʰ the first American soldier has crossed the border into German territory and by 12ᵗʰ September several tank and infantry units advance into Germany along a front between Aachen and Luxembourg, reaching Roetgen, a few kilometres south of Aachen. Hitherto the German population has experienced the force of its enemies primarily from the air. Theatres of war have been distant from German territory. Soon the foe will be confronted face to face. The *Westwall*, a formidable belt of interconnected pillboxes and bunkers, has been breached in several places. One of the soldiers who crosses into Germany that day is the young Ernest Hemingway, working as a war correspondent. Enemy forces have reached the outer wooded areas of Aachen and occupy a hill overlooking the city, site of the *Pelzerturm*, from where they have an unencumbered view and can direct shells and artillery fire straight in.

General von Schwerin, appointed to overall command of the city, has arrived with divisions in retreat from France and takes stock of the situation from his headquarters in the Quellenhof. He is a much-decorated commander, admired by Hitler, but now disillusioned with the regime, and observes the streets in chaos as evacuating citizens compete with troops ordered to take up new defensive positions. On the 13ᵗʰ he issues orders to halt the evacuation and composes a hand-written letter of capitulation to the American commander in English to avoid more senseless bloodshed. He asks them to spare the city and its inhabitants; they could now take it with a minimum loss of life. Estimates vary as to how many civilians are still in the city; there may be around 25,000. He expects the Americans to respond and march in the following day and has the letter delivered to the telegraph office in the centre of the city, which has been ordered to keep functioning until enemy troops arrive.

But events follow an unexpected course. The anticipated imminent advance of American forces into Aachen stalls. On the 14th, General von Schwerin is ordered to start a defence of the city, new divisions arrive and the first phase of the Battle of Aachen begins. He tries in vain to retrieve his note from the telegraph office but it has already been passed on and falls into the hands of the SS, as a result of which he is relieved of duties and replaced. Von Schwerin is arrested and later has to answer for his actions before a war tribunal, but is pardoned by Hitler, narrowly escaping the death penalty. He will spend the final phase of the war in 1945 as a prisoner of the British. In the post-war era, his actions in Aachen will be subject to intense scrutiny and changing historical interpretation. Is he truly acting in the interests of the population and the city?

◆◆◆

Minny and Berta are at Kaisersruh in a state of heightened tension and indecision. They fear for their lives as news has reached them that German borders have been breached by the Allies. Although propaganda has impressed upon them that any enemy will show no mercy, the general view is that it is preferable to fall into the hands of Americans than Russians. There is a rumour that American soldiers "carry knives to scalp German civilians in the old Indian style!" Berta, usually strong and decisive, is dazed by events and receives an offer to evacuate, from the Zintzen family at the farm next door. She accepts, but does not try to persuade Minny, who is stubborn and has always promised herself she would not abandon her home, to accompany her. In her youth and naiveté, Minny does not recognise the dangers of staying put. Throughout the war the Zintzen and Rössler families have become mutually supportive, sharing cramped space in the air-raid bunkers and exchanging farm produce for other bartered commodities.

Brother Erhard's whereabouts are unknown. Berta fetches Emil's black, metal-cornered travelling trunk from the attic, which has remained undamaged by the bombing, and she hastily fills it with clothes, a few remaining valuables and a bulky bale of dark woollen cloth, which might be useful for bartering. Its travels will now be dictated by the progress and aftermath of the war. It is loaded, along with a suitcase stuffed with bedding, on to a farm cart. The youngest four of the Zintzen's six children climb aboard another cart and sit amongst luggage and bulky feather duvets with red and white checked covers, waving cheerfully to Minny as the horses pull out of the yard. Their destination is Frau Zintzen's parents' farm at Gey, a small hamlet near Düren, a distance of about twenty kilometres to the northeast. Minny notes the address, but they have no idea when or where they will meet again.

Streams of refugees pass by the estate on the steep main road out of the city, taking matters into their own hands after "official" evacuation procedures have stalled and been aborted, then restarted. Word has spread that there is room to rest at Kaisersruh, and families trudge up the drive, with babies, terrified whimpering children of various ages, and possessions hastily loaded into prams and handcarts. They are seeking shelter and water to wash in, settling in the outhouses and garages. Now Emil's instructions on how to slaughter and gut chickens are put to use, as Minny cooks large pots of nourishing chicken soup with whatever vegetables she can still scavenge, to feed everyone.

She weighs up options in her mind. Should she stay and continue to offer shelter to passing refugees? Here at least she might be useful. Herr Zintzen, who along with other local farmers in protected occupations is permitted to stay and tend his animals, has made her the offer of keeping house for him, now that his wife has gone. Minny is not sure of his motives.

She could also take up the offer of fleeing with the *Wehrbezirkskommando*, who have similarly offered protection. She naively thinks that in staying, she might be able to save her beloved home - but from what? Confusion and uncertainty are exacerbated by the continuous dull echoes of shelling, as the city is surrounded and bombarded by American forces.

The Nellessens' car stands abandoned in their garage, as the family has moved to relatives in Holland. Had Minny learned to drive before the war, she could have used it to flee until petrol ran out. The only option is by bicycle. Noise of shelling gets louder as districts on the Kaisersruh side of the city are repeatedly targeted. Stray shots and shells land near Kaisersruh. In the last week of September she decides to evacuate with the remaining members of the *Wehrbezirks-kommando*.

Into a small leather suitcase she crams clothes, shoes, a few photographs, letters from Hans, and a set of silver cutlery, a confirmation present from Frau Nellessen. The case is strapped to the back of the bicycle; her pet dachshund Raudi, from whom she cannot bear to be parted, rides in the front basket. So far he has survived the air raids, even disappearing into the woods for days and emerging unscathed. He is the last tie with home. Minny secures the doors and windows of their house and lowers the wooden shutters, but they are weakened by bombing and it would not be difficult to force them open. A small number of refugees are still sheltering and have not yet moved on, but she decides it is unwise to wait any longer.

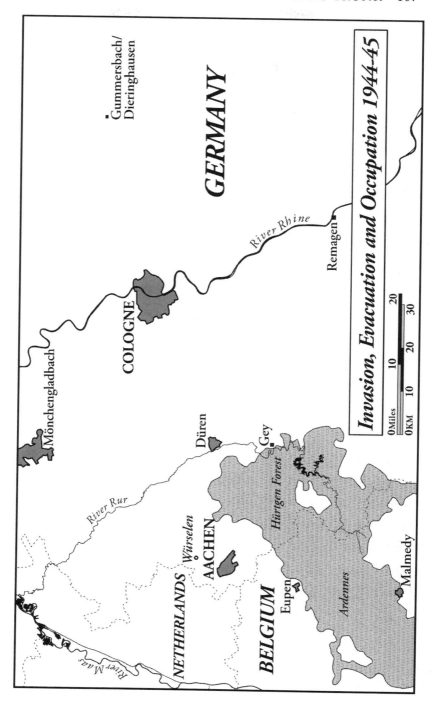

Invasion, Evacuation and Occupation 1944–45

GERMANY

Gummersbach/
Dieringhausen

River Rhine

Remagen

COLOGNE

Mönchengladbach

Düren

Gey

Hürtgen Forest

River Rur

NETHERLANDS

Würselen

AACHEN

BELGIUM

Eupen

Ardennes

Malmedy

River Maas

0 Miles   10   20
0 KM   10   20   30

Hitler's resolve is hardened. On the 19ᵗʰ he orders his commanders to resist the American advance, in what will be called the Battle of Hürtgen Forest, causing more senseless loss of life in what would constitute part of a final stand in the West. In the dense conifer forests between the Rur river and Aachen, south west of Düren, there are colossal casualties on both sides; the slaughter will last until the following February, and the offensive become a byword for desperate, pointless combat. American commanders and troops are unprepared for the harshness of the terrain and the impenetrability of the forests, which are dotted with booby traps and minefields, and crossed by sparse tracks and roads. By contrast, many German soldiers have witnessed combat on the Russian front and are used to snow and falling temperatures as winter sets in.

Mid-September sees continuous and brutal combat in the suburbs and villages around Aachen, with losses and gains on both sides as pockets of German resistance fight on. Many of the German defenders are either teenage boys or middle-aged and elderly men: Hitler's so called national *Volkssturm* (people's militia), in which the last reserves of both young and old are being called up in phases to support *Wehrmacht* troops. It will shortly be put under the overall control of Himmler.

The action in the Hürtgen Forest overlaps with the Battle of Aachen, and is a crucial factor in preventing the Allies from achieving their initial goal of a swift victory and advance through to the Rhine plain before the end of the year. Hitler's commanders are intent on maintaining control of the Rur dam at the head of the Rur reservoir, as the Allied advance might be halted if the waters were released to flood the valley.

 By 21ˢᵗ September there is a lull in the battle for the city and both sides take stock. The initial phase will come to be known as the "First Battle of Aachen". American commanders now decide on a pincer movement around the city.

◆◆◆

Minny sets off in a northerly direction up the hill away from the city of Aachen on a dry, sunny late September afternoon, with a motley group of *Wehrbezirkskommando* employees and their families. Some have left without knowing the fate of family members left behind. It will be another five weeks or so before Aachen finally falls, the first city on German soil to be "conquered" or "liberated", depending on one's perspective. Minny rides stretches by bicycle, but for short distances she jumps on trucks that are accompanying those fleeing, with the bicycle lying beside her amidst office equipment cleared from the Kaisersruh estate house.

As one of the first women in Aachen to wear trousers, she finds that her cycling trousers, tailor made by the family seamstress, now come into their own. There is little idea of where the group is heading or how long they might be travelling. They pass through Würselen, constantly stopping to take cover under the truck or in woods, as enemy planes approach: it is safer to travel in darkness. Fighting on the ground has lessened in intensity as combatants decide on new strategies, but there are ongoing air attacks.

On the first night they reach Alsdorf, a mining village, where she begs a place to sleep at the house of one of the Nellessens' cooks, who is married to a miner and has not yet fled. Others find accommodation in abandoned houses. They beg food from shops still in business, pick unharvested fruit from trees or dig up root vegetables from fields. Scraps must also be found for Raudi. Within weeks, both Alsdorf and Würselen will be occupied by advancing Allied troops as the ring around the city slowly closes.

One night they take shelter in a barn where a woman, who has recently given birth and is obviously weakened and sick, begs them to take her child. The image of her lying in the straw haunts Minny. They cannot help her. The next night they rest in an abandoned factory where the local sweet sticky spread made from sugar beet, known as *Rübenkraut*, has been produced, and they take some tubs.

There is no fixed route; the way depends on roads or tracks being accessible. At Remagen, south of Cologne, they cross the Rhine by the bridge still standing. American forces will not advance to the river, a considerable natural obstacle, until March 1945. Beyond Cologne they enter a hilly district, dotted with small towns, villages and hamlets – *das Bergische Land*.

In Dieringhausen, a village with a railway station, near the small town of Gummersbach, the unit has been assigned shelter. They have been travelling for over a week, with limited washing opportunities and no proper sanitation. Assembling in the school yard, sullen villagers who have no choice in the matter, "select" the dirty and dishevelled newly arrived refugees, contemptuously labelling them *Bombenweiber* – bomb women. Minny is taken by a married couple to their cramped, grimy house and sleeps in a storage room without proper bedclothes, debating how long she can endure.

After some days she decides to try and reach – by whatever means possible – Lohausen, a large airfield on the outskirts of Düsseldorf on the east bank of the River Rhine, where she had learned from colleagues at work in Aachen of a huge underground bunker complex, providing shelter. She is still technically in police employ and without any clear idea of her motives for leaving, still feels under obligation to follow orders. She sets off alone from Dieringhausen, leaving Raudi in the care of the *Wehrbezirkskommando*. It is a distance of about forty kilometers which she covers by hitching rides in *Wehrmacht* trucks transporting the wounded, or riding on tanks.

On reaching Lohausen, Minny experiences her lowest point and rests for some days. Her family is scattered, she is physically weak and uncertain as to what she is hoping to accomplish. She cannot explain her feelings of loyalty to her employers. An old inefficient stove provides meagre heating against the cold. It is clear she cannot be of use so she decides to search for her mother, last glimpsed heading off from Kaisersruh on a cart with Frau Zintzen, bound for her parents' farm at Gey, near Düren.

This journey too takes several days. Once again, the Rhine has to be crossed. She rests in abandoned buildings, travelling by night as air attacks are frequent. No one can be trusted. As she approaches Gey in darkness, she is barely aware of intensifying action in the Hürtgen Forest to the south east.

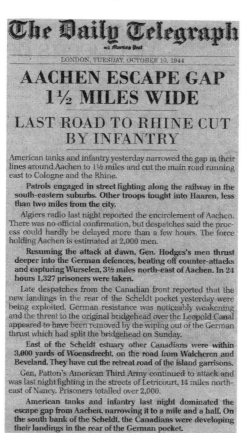

The Daily Telegraph
and Morning Post
LONDON, TUESDAY, OCTOBER 19, 1944

AACHEN ESCAPE GAP
1½ MILES WIDE

LAST ROAD TO RHINE CUT
BY INFANTRY

American tanks and infantry yesterday narrowed the gap in their lines around Aachen to 1½ miles and cut the main road running east to Cologne and the Rhine.

Patrols engaged in street fighting along the railway in the south-eastern suburbs. Other troops fought into Haaren, less than two miles from the city.

Algiers radio last night reported the encirclement of Aachen. There was no official confirmation, but despatches said the process could hardly be delayed more than a few hours. The force holding Aachen is estimated at 2,000 men.

Resuming the attack at dawn, Gen. Hodges's men thrust deeper into the German defences, beating off counter-attacks and capturing Wurselen, 3½ miles north-east of Aachen. In 24 hours 1,327 prisoners were taken.

Late despatches from the Canadian front reported that the new landings in the rear of the Scheldt pocket yesterday were being exploited. German resistance was noticeably weakening and the threat to the original bridgehead over the Leopold Canal appeared to have been removed by the wiping out of the German thrust which had split the bridgehead on Sunday.

East of the Scheldt estuary other Canadians were within 3,000 yards of Woensdrecht, on the road from Walcheren and Beveland. They have cut the retreat road of the island garrisons.

Gen. Patton's American Third Army continued to attack and was last night fighting in the streets of Letricourt, 14 miles north-east of Nancy. Prisoners totalled over 2,000.

American tanks and infantry last night dominated the escape gap from Aachen, narrowing it to a mile and a half. On the south bank of the Scheldt, the Canadians were developing their landings in the rear of the German pocket.

In Aachen in the first week of October the slaughter has begun anew, and is widely reported in the British and American press. In view of the September lull, it will come to be known as the "Second Battle of Aachen".

American forces drop thousands of flyers over the city, demanding unconditional surrender from commanders and population, and making no bones about the almost complete encirclement of the city. Waves of bombs and artillery pound the urban areas.

Concurrently, the Battle of Overloon is fought on the flat lowlands of the Southern Netherlands north of Aachen, between German and Allied tanks, as Montgomery, in "Operation Market Garden", attempts to secure a further corridor through the area in a push towards the Rhine. Hitler's resources are stretched to the limit.

US infantry, Aachen 15th October 1944

The two flanks of the pincer around Aachen finally close on 16th October in the vicinity of Kaisersruh. There has been vicious combat in the areas around Würselen and Haaren. The city centre is being fought for street by street, as German commanders follow orders to "defend it to the last man" and withdraw to the Quellenhof as headquarters, and then finally to a bunker in the Rütscherstrasse. In the nearby Belgian town of Verviers, top Allied military representatives convene to discuss the fate of the first German city to fall. President Eisenhower is represented by Generals Bradley, Hodges and Patton, the

British by Field Marshal Montgomery and King George VI himself.

Battle of Aachen, October 1944

On 20th October Aachen is taken after a last desperate bloody stand. Oberst Wilck signs the declaration of surrender on the 21st. He is taken captive and flown to London for interrogation, after which he will spend three years as a prisoner of the British.

US casualty, Aachen October 1944

◆◆◆

Minny and her mother are ignorant of their city's fate, which would in any case be strangely irrelevant, as personal concerns are uppermost and occupy most waking hours. By repeatedly asking for directions, Minny locates the isolated farm buildings on the edge of Gey at night. Berta is sheltering with the Zintzen family in a cramped cellar lit by flickering candles and is astonished to see Minny turning up unexpectedly. Neither knew for certain the other was still alive. They agree it is preferable to attempt a return to Dieringhausen, although constant echoes from the intensifying American offensive in the nearby Hürtgen forest are a reminder of ongoing danger. The Zintzen family will also soon take the decision to move further inland out of the battle zone. Berta has several heavy pieces of luggage, including the bulky trunk transported there by horse and cart, so she hastily gathers lighter items in a small case, and they leave the next morning, abandoning the trunk, once again begging rides from passing army vehicles. Back in Dieringhausen Berta is found a room with a family who run a small garden nursery. But the household where Minny had previously slept is unwilling to accommodate her and she moves in with Berta, sleeping on the floor, wrapped in an old fur-lined army coat saved from Emil's First World War service.

From the window of their room, Minny spots an old deck chair, which she carries into the house; this serves as her bed for the coming months. When she announces she is attempting the journey back to Gey to fetch the trunk, she confronts disbelief from Berta, who thinks her mad! However, as it contains their only remaining worldly goods which might be key to survival in the approaching winter, she is adamant. A courier from the *Wehrbezirkskommando*, Herr Schreiner, who has a functioning motorcycle and roomy sidecar, offers transport. He drives her back across the Rhine to Gey to retrieve the trunk and leaves her at a railway station to complete the journey.

A goods train arrives. Minny jumps on and drags the trunk and an additional heavy suitcase beside her. But the train is targeted by low-flying Allied aircraft and shudders to a halt. Minny hurls herself off, throws herself onto the tracks between the wheels and crouches in terror, praying. She emerges, trembling, surrounded by corpses and the wounded as several wagons have been hit. She remounts the train to search for belongings and a fellow passenger helps salvage the trunk and suitcase. Sirens can be heard, as ambulances are on their way to help the wounded. By once again hitching rides and begging lifts on trucks from German troops, she miraculously makes it back to Dieringhausen unscathed - with the rescued trunk and suitcase.

German POWs, Aachen, October 1944

It is late October. The battle for Aachen is at an end, but hostilities will continue to rage until the following May, costing hundreds of thousands more lives on both sides. Aachen's ultimate fate is barely mentioned in the German written news or daily broadcast *Wehrmacht* reports, which cloak the facts of its demise in phrases describing continuous heavy fighting and heroic resistance. For the Allies, though, the fall of the city is a psychological triumph, widely reported in the British and American media. American units which have already established a foothold in Germany report that the population of Aachen greeted their arrival with mixed responses ranging from "complacent, submissive and obedient to cooperative and grateful".

As refugees start trickling back to a shattered city, a mere week after the capitulation, on 31st October, American occupiers swear in a provisional puppet city administration, headed by lawyer Franz Oppenhoff, who appoints nine German councillors to help in the difficult task of administering a shaky and totally uncharted peace. As the weather deteriorates, inexperienced American troops continue to encounter fierce resistance in the intensifying Hürtgen Forest fighting.

◆◆◆

Emil has discovered his family's whereabouts through Tante Lydia in Neckarsteinach. He now writes to Minny and Berta in Dieringhausen in November to say that he has been given leave, and arrives for a short visit. Even in these desperate times, postal services function and trains run spasmodically, although, as Minny has witnessed, railway lines are an obvious and continued target for Allied aircraft. They all occupy one narrow room, water is limited, most of the time they smell unwashed and feel grimy. The days are completely taken up with searching out food, which is shared with the family in whose house they are billeted. Everyone cooks on the same stove, the sole source of heat in the house. Minny is resentful

118 · INGRID DIXON

that their host family makes little effort to barter for food, leaving her to ride from farm to farm, muffled in scarves as winter approaches, exchanging what she can. Apple trees in the garden provide late autumn fruit and a nearby bakery is still supplying *Kommissbrot*.

Word gets around that horsemeat is available nearby, as soldiers have abandoned animals to their fate. This has never been part of their diet, but they are so hungry that Minny takes her place in the queue, bartering with cigarettes, which a member of the *Wehrbezirkskommando* has brought from Aachen, where he owned a tobacconist shop. The smell of cooking horse meat in the kitchen is so overpowering it prevents her from swallowing any. A goods train carrying coal is stranded in the vicinity, unable to carry on after an air attack. Minny and others seek it out, clambering over mounds of coal, filling as many sacks as can be balanced on a bicycle, and pedalling back with difficulty. It is backbreaking work.

As winter approaches they are thankful for the extra clothing stored in the trunk. The *Wehrbezirkskommando* has moved into a building in the village, and she helps with office work and administration, typing and filing. She thankfully brings Raudi back to their billet. The area they have been assigned to has rolling hills, woods and fields, but they are too preoccupied with basic survival to find respite in the countryside.

Without access to a radio, reports of German victories or Allied setbacks which reach their ears second hand must be viewed with scepticism. The port of Antwerp, to the north in Belgium, has been in Allied hands since the first week of September, and is vital in enabling reinforcements to supply the advance on a broad front towards the Rhine, but this is being hampered by continuous German resistance, in the form of rocket attacks throughout the late autumn of 1944. General Walter Model broadcasts a message of encouragement to troops on 9th November, commemorating those who died at the *Feldherrnhalle*, in 1923, in which Hitler and his followers participated in a failed coup attempt.

> *"The enemy's attempts to break through our front with strong forces at Arnhem, west of Venlo, at Aachen, and south of Trier, collapsed against the firm resistance of .... Divisions".*

In reality, the British have launched a brutal new wave of air attacks, Operation Queen, reducing Düren, Jülich and Heinsberg, and numerous smaller towns and villages in the region of Aachen, to piles of rubble, as part of the continued Allied thrust east to the Rur river. By the end of November, American units encircle and enter the village of Hürtgen, whose name will become attached to the battle as a whole.

On 11th December Minny gets a surprise and welcome visit from Anita, who was evacuated from Aachen shortly before Minny fled, and is staying with relatives nearby, near Overath. She is on her way to Erfurt, a considerable distance to the east, where, even at this late stage, she has been sent for further training in communication and intelligence skills. The sole of her shoe is disintegrating, so they repair it with cardboard.

Anita at Police School, 1944

♦♦♦

The areas around Düren and Gey experience fierce combat as American troops advance. On 16th December, Hitler launches his long planned Ardennes Offensive, usually known in German as the Rundstedt Offensive. Its code-name is *Wacht am Rhein* (Watch on the Rhine).

For Hitler, the name "Ardennes" has an almost mythical resonance; in 1940 German troops were able to push through the area to occupy France with unprecedented speed. Now the aim is to advance over the river Maas (Meuse), and reach Antwerp, to cut off Allied supply routes. Hitler concentrates all available troops and resources on his final gamble. In its initial phases he has the element of surprise on his side, as intelligence indicators are not heeded.

Combat rages in the densely wooded terrain south of Aachen, along the border between Germany, and Belgium and Luxembourg, encompassing the Eifel area to the south of Aachen, where in former days Minny along with fellow Aacheners had hiked and enjoyed excursions to picture-postcard towns of cobbled streets and half-timbered buildings. In the English-speaking world the offensive will come to be known as the "Battle of the Bulge", as German units attempt to penetrate the advancing Allied front and force it back in a "Bulge" towards the west. It will last until the end of January 1945, in public consciousness virtually eclipsing the battle in the Hürtgen Forest, which for German forces served as a staging post for the offensive in the Ardennes.

Hitler reassures his military advisers that, confident of success in the Ardennes, his goal is to retake Aachen, where an eerie quiet now reigns. By Christmas, American occupiers have established a department to start taking stock of the devastation, and a limited number of buildings have been made habitable, hampered by an acute lack of manpower and building materials, to say nothing of heavy equipment to shift rubble. Christmas Mass is celebrated in the cathedral, attended by a handful of American soldiers.

A city architect has been appointed by mayor Oppenhoff to oversee repairs to the damaged cathedral and valuable works of art are supposedly "secured" and protected, but individuals amongst occupying American troops consider the looting and confiscation of portable art works their legitimate right.

◆◆◆

Erhard has managed to obtain a few days' leave from his unit, now stationed in Hamburg, and hitches rides to Dieringhausen for a subdued Christmas. A photo shows him standing in the snow before returning to duty. There is seemingly not yet an end to the nightmare. At least last year they were still in their home. A low point has been reached. It is freezing and damp; every day is a struggle. In addition, letters that Minny has been sending from Dieringhausen to Hans on the Eastern Front have been returned marked *vermisst* (missing). Her feelings are ambivalent. Hans has always expressed a desire to marry her before the end of the war, but she had been unable seriously to contemplate a future with him. Nevertheless, she is devastated.

16-year old Erhard in uniform, Christmas 1944

By the end of the year there is stalemate in the Ardennes. Hitler has staked everything on this final counter-offensive, which leads to a surge in German morale but whose outcome is by no means certain.

CHAPTER SIX

Preparation

Whilst the British public were being informed in radio broadcasts and newspapers of the progress of hostilities, a parallel clandestine war of intelligence and counter-intelligence, agents and saboteurs was being waged, whose story could only be told decades later.

Jim was reluctantly drawn into this sphere in 1941. The eldest of three children from Liverpool, he might have stayed in the Royal Artillery, where he first served after being called up in 1940, but for one significant fact. In spite of having left school at 16, he was a gifted self-taught and natural linguist, speaking French, German and Dutch almost fluently, with a working knowledge of several other languages.

The Intelligence Corps was seeking to recruit personnel with skills in relevant European tongues and must have noted his competence, rightly judging it was wasted in the Royal Artillery. Soon after joining up, Jim was attached to the Intelligence Corps at the Field Security Centre in Winchester where, after training, he stayed for a year. He was a dutiful if unenthusiastic soldier, who never aspired to a commission, and was relieved to be released from military duty when discharged, boasting that he never gave anything beyond that which was expected of him.

The Intelligence Corps had been formed in July 1940, integrating and consolidating disparate and *ad hoc* intelligence and security units that existed to that point. Numerous so-called Field Security Sections were constituted throughout the following months, each unit consisting of ten to fifteen officers and other ranks, which operated in support of the British Army in numerous theatres of war until hostilities ceased, and in occupied areas after the final total capitulation of May 1945 (see Historical Note 3)

By 1942 Jim was back in Liverpool, where he had spent his childhood and been educated and where his parents and sister still lived. Now he could be billeted at home for a while. Liverpool's extensive dock area had experienced its own Blitz - his unit was responsible for ensuring the security of naval crews and for questioning merchant seamen visiting the port, screening them for possible activity as German agents. Much unofficial undercover work was conducted in the pubs around the docklands.

Composite panorama of bomb-damaged Liverpool, circa 1942

As Operation Overlord – the landings in Normandy – was being planned in the spring of 1944, Allied armies were secretly assembling and training near the English south coast. Field Security Sections in the coastal areas of Devon and Cornwall were responsible for ensuring the security of the invasion plans. Jim's experience in port security at Liverpool now led to a move. He was transferred to a Home Port Security Section in Plymouth in early 1944, working in the Torquay area.

As the massed Allied armies implemented the D-Day invasion of 6th June 1944 and advanced across Northwest Europe, Field Security Sections operated in support, searching for saboteurs and collaborators, and establishing security behind the front line. Jim was first sent to locations in Belgium and by October was in the port of Antwerp, which had been captured on 4th September by British units of Montgomery's 21st Army Group. The approaches to the port were left vulnerable, however, and supply lines were subjected to continuous counter-attacks by German V1 cruise missiles and V2 rockets throughout the autumn months. Jim's parents listened in trepidation to reports of the attacks on the radio.

But time spent in Antwerp was to be short-lived, for in November he was transferred to 64 Field Security Section, a move which would alter the course of his future life. 64 FSS was unusual. One of three units formed to maintain the security of the Special Operations Executive, the secret organization formed by Churchill in 1940 to drop agents into occupied Europe, it supported and organised resistance movements. Jim's knowledge of French, German and Dutch were put to use as the unit worked with other FS sections behind enemy lines in undercover and sensitive assignments, shortly before the start of the Ardennes counter-offensive, searching for collaborators, infiltrators and saboteurs, and interrogating captured prisoners. In addition, he was probably involved in tracing and rescuing Allied agents behind German lines and debriefing Dutch agents sent across the lines to gain intelligence. He never divulged details of these activities in later years.

Information is tantalisingly scant, but from papers still extant in the Overlord Intelligence and Security files, it can be deduced that in the closing weeks of 1944, 64 FSS - with Jim - was based in the village of Horst in Holland, just a few kilometres from the front line demarcated by the river Maas (Meuse), and remained there until the spring. A counter-intelligence report of 28th February 1945, relating to plans for the German/Dutch frontier, states:

> *"The control line behind forward troops going into Germany has been taken over by one of the FS Sections, which will eventually be allotted to frontier control on the German frontier......They are assisted by several companies of the Netherlands Grenzwacht (frontier control) which will also move up later to the German frontier".*

Although not named, it is probable this refers to Jim's unit, 64 FSS. Within weeks, in March, 21st Army Group fought their way across the Rhine and continued their advance into Germany, spurred on by Montgomery's words, read to troops in February:

> *"We know our enemy well; we must expect him to fight hard to stave off defeat, possibly in the vain hope that we may crack before he does. But we shall not crack; we shall see this thing through to the end."*

Jim and his unit entered Germany in the wake of the Allied advance, as Minny and Berta waited in trepidation in Dieringhausen, still a relatively comfortable distance east of the Allied front.

CHAPTER SEVEN

1945: Occupation

Even as evacuees east of the Rhine, Minny and Berta were subjected to repeated air attacks in the early months of 1945. German resistance in the Ardennes and continuing Allied advances towards the natural barrier of the Rhine ensured constant danger from supporting Allied aircraft, which launched waves of bomber aircraft to disrupt ground supply lines and wear down the population.

Allied troops in Hürtgen Forest, January 1945

Seeking shelter in the village bunker on a winter night during an air raid warning, Berta slipped on a patch of ice in the dark and injured her thumb, which became swollen and infected, refusing to heal. After a few weeks it was amputated at a makeshift hospital in nearby Ründeroth.

Berta 1945

With increasing shortages, patients received very little food. Minny cycled every day from Dieringhausen with extra provisions, riding carefully on icy roads and hilly terrain to avoid skidding. As she repeatedly fell from the bicycle, several hours of daylight each day were taken up; it seemed that life consisted of nothing but searching for and delivering food.

By the end of January, the local *Aachener Nachrichten* newspaper resumed production in the city, sponsored by the American "Psychological Warfare Division", which launched a fact-finding mission in Aachen, monitoring and reporting on the morale and mental attitudes of the German population. A Jewish German-speaking American of Austrian descent, Saul Padover, assigned to the project, would publish a book on his findings after the war, analysing the conflicting sentiments experienced by the people of Aachen under occupation, which would be mirrored by those in the remaining Reich after the total capitulation in May.

East of the Rhine in Dieringhausen, however, only sporadic printed news was getting through. As the Allies gained the upper hand in the Ardennes offensive, it was clear by 25th January that Hitler had lost his last gamble. Ardennes commander Walter Model committed suicide rather than surrender and violate a personal oath to Hitler to fight to the death. News of Allied bombings of towns on the Lower Rhine towards the border with Holland, the Roman city of Xanten, Goch and Kleve, home to Henry VIII's fourth wife Anne of Cleves, followed by Dresden in the east in February, filtered through to Minny and Berta by word of mouth. On 10th February, the Hürtgen Forest offensive was considered at an end, as the Allies secured the strategically crucial Rur dam, but not before German resistance succeeded in jamming open the floodgates, releasing torrents of water down the river along the Rur valley, delaying by two more weeks an Allied advance to the Rhine. 33,000 American soldiers had sacrificed their lives in the battle, and almost an equal number of German troops.

As Berta recovered from the amputation of her thumb, she learned to hold objects and write using four fingers on her right hand. Crocheting, a lifelong passion, would have to be mastered afresh. They received a message by post that Emil, guarding prisoners-of-war at Soest in Westphalia, was permitted visitors. It was a considerable distance to the north, taking several hours by train, but still a relatively safe distance east of the advancing Allied front, enabling travel. They took Raudi, to lift Emil's spirits. But Raudi was no longer welcome in the household that was temporarily sheltering them. While waiting at a freezing and deserted country railway station on the return journey, a forester approached them. "I'll take him off your hands," he offered. Heartbroken, they agreed. There was no alternative. A few weeks later the forester wrote to say Raudi refused to eat, pined away and died.

As the Allies convened to deliberate strategies in their ultimate spring push towards the Rhine, combat zones were drawing ever nearer to Dieringhausen. On 6th March American tanks were standing in front of the cathedral at Cologne. The Rhine was crossed on 7th March at Remagen and, weakened by continuous military activity, the bridge collapsed into the river on the 17th. British and American troops, however, were already advancing on a broad front. Between Wesel on the lower Rhine and south of Remagen, two flanks of Allied units gradually drew together in a pincer movement, which converged in the first week of April, forming what was known as the *Ruhrkessel* – the Ruhr pocket – trapping hundreds of thousands of *Wehrmacht* troops and civilians. Gradually the circle was drawn in as Allied units advanced into the pocket. Unknown to them, Minny and Berta were caught near its southern boundary. American infantrymen marched into Gummersbach on 11th April, and a large field on the outskirts of the town was hastily put to use to confine thousands of surrendering and captured German soldiers. During these final weeks in Dieringhausen, Minny and Berta were strangely unaware of the progress of enemy gains and their implications, until a *Wehrbezirkskommando* colleague called on Minny, informing her that the few remaining serving soldiers of the unit, including himself, had no option but to give themselves up. In a token of farewell he left a green enamel Art Deco clock from the 1930s.

In the final death throes of the Reich, as units were disbanded and order collapsed, countless German soldiers sought to evade capture and seek a way home amidst the chaos of a deteriorating situation. Erhard, caught in the maelstrom and no longer feeling under obligation to his military masters, decided to chance his luck in this way, but not before he too was held by Allied troops. His anti-aircraft unit of 16-year-olds, hastily convened in Aachen in August 1944, had been moved to the Hürtgen Forest in September, and then to Hamburg by the end of 1944. By March he was in southern Germany, in an area known as the Spessart in Franconia, northern Bavaria.

The region witnessed American forces encountering serious resistance to their swift advance after crossing the Rhine, and many towns and villages were occupied only after considerable loss of life on both sides. What motivated *Wehrmacht* soldiers to fight on, sacrificing their last reserves in the knowledge of certain and unavoidable defeat? Historians will debate this question for decades to come. A complex mix of factors was at play: many were driven on by feelings of intense patriotism and a desire to protect the fatherland, nurtured through years of indoctrination, which spurred them on in spite of the realisation that the *Führer* and his regime had led the German people to destruction. Yet others were spurred on at learning of the declared Allied intent not to accept anything less than Germany's total and unconditional surrender. A sense of honour motivated others to die fighting rather than to be shot for desertion or disobeying orders.

Erhard's unit of frightened and demoralised teenage boys was surrounded and captured by American soldiers. At Bad Orb, a spa town which was the site of a notorious prisoner-of-war camp holding American soldiers captured in the Ardennes, Erhard was pushed into a queue outside the parish hall, where prisoners were being processed. The soldiers may have thought they were to be issued with an *Entlassungsschein* – a certificate of discharge from the *Wehrmacht* – but Erhard sensed that the dishevelled group would be transported into holding camps along with hundreds of thousands of their compatriots taken into custody during those weeks. Into his pocket he had thrust a flyer, one of thousands distributed by the Allies exhorting *Wehrmacht* soldiers to give themselves up. Taking advantage of the noisy confusion surrounding him, Erhard slipped away, risking being shot, resolved to seek a way through to Dieringhausen, where he knew Minny and Berta to be living as evacuees.

On a dark moonless night, he buried his identification tag, uniform and *Soldbuch* (Army paybook) in a field. The oval pale grey base metal tag was divided on its surface by a line of perforation along which it could be bent and broken into two, with his Army identification number stamped on both halves. Next day a sympathetic farmer provided him with dusty second-hand civilian clothes. Reaching Dieringhausen after two weeks on the road, having evaded detection, he related his experiences to Minny and Berta. Good Friday – 30th March – he described as "the worst day of my life". Before capture, his company had come under fire after retreating to and sheltering in a bunker. He narrowly escaped death but several of his compatriots were not so lucky. But he had never been "officially" released from duty, nor received a certificate of discharge from either side. This was surreptitiously acquired by Minny for him in Dieringhausen from the *Wehrbezirks-kommando*, just before it dissolved. The unit and Minny's family had been mutually supportive in the acquisition of food and transport and dissemination of information. Their disband-ment increased feelings of insecurity and bewilderment.

Throughout Germany, the final weeks of the Third Reich were marked by an intensifying series of murderous acts instigated by the regime, which would come to be known as *Endphaseverbrechen* - crimes perpetrated in the final phase of the war. Aachen city mayor Oppenhoff, appointed by American occupiers the previous October, had expressed fears for his life on taking office, which proved justified; he was assassinated on

25th March by a so-called "Werewolf" commando under orders from Himmler. It was a sober reminder to the people of Aachen that, even in times of Allied military control, German resistance and the collapsing Nazi state could still deliver a fatal blow.

In the closing days of April and the first days of May 1945, without newspapers or a radio, Minny and her family in Dieringhausen received scant information, second hand, and intuition or wishful thinking guided them what to believe or doubt. People acknowledged events only when faced with their irrefutable reality and shut out what was unpalatable. Details of the final bloody defeat of the country were gradually pieced together in fragments over many months and years. The closing chapters of the war – the meeting of Soviet and Allied troops on the banks of the Elbe near Torgau on 25th April, briefly united in the achievement of a common goal, and the demise of the Third Reich after the final brutal battle for Berlin – were almost irrelevant, overshadowed by efforts for day-to-day survival in the Rössler family's location, far from Berlin.

Minny cannot even recall hearing of the alleged death of Adolf Hitler on 29th April in the bunker in Berlin, the appointment of Admiral Dönitz, named in the *Führer's* will as his successor as head of government, or the official surrender of remaining German troops in Holland and Northern Germany to Field Marshal Bernard Montgomery on 4th May at his headquarters near Lüneburg. The final unconditional surrender of 7th May was signed in Rheims in Eisenhower's headquarters. Its practical considerations and legal parameters were unprecedented in their complexity. Questions of war reparations and the establishment of the boundaries of post-war Germany would lead to years of wrangling.

Amongst the tangle of rumours, half-truths and suppositions reaching Dieringhausen, it was suggested refugees might try to return home. Whilst an end to hostilities reported in the first week of May brought relief, it also raised more unanswerable questions: what now? Home? Was it still standing? What transport could be found? An army driver, forced by injury to retire from active service, had commandeered a truck and let it be known he would try and find a route through to Aachen and the surrounding villages, but at a price. A group of refugees who were willing to attempt the journey, and more importantly, who were able to pay in kind, quickly accepted the offer. They included Minny, Berta and Erhard. The driver negotiated his payment from everyone before setting off – from Berta a small piece of gold jewellery and the bale of dark woollen cloth that she had hung on to for such an eventuality.

There were no formal goodbyes, no niceties or promises to keep in touch. They were as thankful to leave the household that had been forced to shelter them temporarily, as their "hosts" were glad to witness their departure. As they prepared to leave, groups of former prisoners of the Germans, released from labour camps, roamed the countryside, threatening German civilians with small daggers and looting whatever they could find.

The trunk was once more filled with their remaining dirty, well-worn bedding and clothing, and hauled up into the back of the truck. The random group of travellers was united only by a desire to return "home", by a hope that there was something to return to. The journey lasted over a week; today the distance could be covered in a few hours.

Vehicles of all types in varying states of repair stood abandoned for the taking, but a lack of fuel prevented most being used. However, the truck which was to transport them didn't run on petrol. It was fuelled by wood. They had never come across this sort of vehicle before.

Piled up on the back, open to the sky, alongside the cargo of people and assorted baggage, was a stack of logs. The driver stopped at intervals, everyone jumped off to replenish the pile of wood with what could be scavenged at the roadside, and the engine was stoked with logs. A large funnel belched clouds of dark smoke as they travelled. At night they burrowed amongst the luggage for bedding and slept under the stars on the vehicle. Bushes and woodland afforded the only privacy. Before leaving, they had put aside some bread and sausage for the journey. Minny's suitcase, containing clothing and shoes, and the bicycle on which she had fled ahead of advancing American troops lay beside her on the truck next to the trunk.

Reichstag building, Berlin, 1945

The weeks of May were characterised by widespread chaos and uncertainty, as the former German state ceased to exist, after the final capitulation on 8th May, and was gradually dismantled. Remaining government institutions were declared invalid, military commanders and members of Hitler's government were variously taken into custody or took their own lives, and a tentative framework of military and administrative structures began to be put in place, with new chains of Allied command. Against this background, the dazed, defeated and disorientated German population and millions of displaced refugees had to carry on eking out a living day by day amidst destroyed infrastructure and homes, an absence of any coherent law and order, and unprecedented food and fuel shortages. This time would come to be known as *Stunde Null* – zero hour – when everything was swept away and new beginnings had to be forged in all spheres of national and personal life.

Erhard describes the period as a *Lücke* – a gap or hiatus. The Allies had achieved their goal of total capitulation and had from as early as 1943 onwards, and at the conference at Yalta in February of that year, defined principles on which they envisaged Germany should be governed, but the terms and practicalities of what was to fill the void of a shattered country were to a great extent still nebulous. Policies of occupation were not discussed and formulated in detail until the Potsdam Conference in late July and early August, discussions which, even at an early stage, brought into focus deep divisions quickly becoming apparent between the Soviet Union and its Allies (see Historical Note 4).

As the Rössler family travelled back to Aachen, efforts and thoughts focused on practical matters. Would they reach home? What would be found there? What of the future? Who had survived, who had died? Where might there be food available? Conversation *en route* centred on personal concerns, everyone in the same situation of doubt and uncertainty. Berta suddenly let out a cry, discovering that a battered bag had slipped off into the road. The driver stopped - she ran back to recover it. No-one objected to a short delay as everyone knew what it meant to lose what few belongings were left. Unbeknown to them, their destination of Aachen was now in the newly created British Zone, whose first military Commander-in-Chief and Military Governor was Field Marshal Montgomery.

Although aerial bombing had stopped, the truck was constantly faced with its effects. Most roads were destroyed; at best they were scarred and pitted. They jolted around holes and troughs, wove past the twisted remains of equipment and tanks. Dead horses and human corpses lay everywhere. Spring sunshine warmed them as they travelled, but the stench of death was overwhelming. Columns of refugees threaded their way through the countryside, dragging carts and old prams laden with household goods. From a distance one evening, under cover, Minny watched American soldiers dancing around a camp fire; she noticed that some of them were black, unlike the *Wehrmacht* soldiers she had known.

The hilly landscape of the region where they had sheltered as evacuees slowly gave way to the flatter countryside of the Rhine plain near Cologne, which had fallen to the Allies in early March. Its ancient cathedral was still standing defiantly against the skyline, severely damaged.

Once more they approached the river at Remagen, south of Cologne, but the Ludendorff bridge, which previously had spanned the river and which German troops had repeatedly tried to destroy to prevent Allied troops from crossing, had collapsed; parts were visible in the water. Minny recalls the feeling of desperation at the realisation that a possible route back home was cut off. American soldiers had erected pontoon bridges, and were controlling columns of troops of both vanquished and victors, passing in both directions. A huge camp housing 350,000 German soldiers taken into captivity had been established in the vicinity of the river near Remagen – the *Rheinwiesenlager* – Rhine meadows camp.   Groups of civilian refugees had low priority.   They waited several days by the truck without shelter or sanitation before they were allowed across, but not before being unceremoniously deloused with a white, unpleasant-smelling powder.

With no maps or remaining signposts, a route could only be guessed at.   Nearing Aachen, familiar landmarks, buildings and church spires should have signalled journey's end and lifted spirits.   But Düren, Eschweiler, Jülich, small towns in the region of Aachen, were reduced to heaps of rubble.   Tracks were bulldozed through tons of fallen debris.   Düren was later recorded as having suffered the greatest proportion of destroyed buildings from Allied bombing in the whole of Germany.   Situated on the north east flank of the Hürtgen Forest, which had taken a terrible toll on both sides in the final months of 1944 and the start of 1945, it was finally occupied by advancing American troops in late February.   As the truck crossed a minor river – the Inde – they realised the devastation around them was what remained of the town.   Nearby Gey, where Berta had sheltered the previous autumn, had similarly suffered major destruction from the air before being taken by ground troops in the final weeks of 1944.

Silently, travelling companions left the vehicle to search for the remains of their homes.   American soldiers in Jeeps were in evidence everywhere, trying to establish order from chaos. They stopped the truck on several occasions, attempted to ask for identification in German and finally communicated by gesturing. Those who still had them dug out identity passes and ration coupons. People wandered the streets dazed, digging in the rubble of neighbours' houses for what they could not find in their own. Pieces of paper, attached precariously to heaps of rubble and teetering piles of bricks, fluttered in the wind, each one a request for information about a missing relative or friend.

US occupation troops, Aachen April 1945

Minny, Berta and Erhard approached their home of Kaisersruh through Würselen, not witnessing at that point the devastation in Aachen, the first city on German soil taken by the Allies. It had been a Pyrrhic victory. Occupied by American forces at the end of October 1944, Aachen was an eerie wasteland, destroyed by Allied bombing and weeks of intense house-to-house fighting in the streets. It had been of little strategic importance militarily, but of huge significance culturally and mythologically.

Aacheners would come to have different perspectives on the final days of hostilities in comparison to Germany as a whole, experiencing two dates as "the end": 21st October 1944 and 8th

May 1945. They were separated by 199 days of "head start", during which the city experienced occupation and the absence of conflict, much earlier than most of Germany. Aachen had become an "experiment" in which to try out Allied policies and principles of occupation and administration for the eventual post-war order. Aacheners were proud that the local *Aachener Nachrichten* newspaper was the first publication on German soil, free from NSDAP control, to report the capitulation of 8th May. Interpretation of the two dates would undergo recognised "phases" of changing perspectives through the coming decades.

The War is Over! Unconditional Surrender!

The buildings on the Kaisersruh estate were just visible through the budding leaves unfolding on the trees on the main road as Minny, Berta and Erhard reached home. Relief at arrival was offset by concerns about Emil, of whose whereabouts they still had no knowledge. The truck stopped; the driver helped unload possessions and bicycle, took his payment in kind and disappeared. The trunk, cases and bags were dragged the remaining distance from the road through the park to the house. Minny's efforts to secure the house had been futile. The heavy oak door was swinging on its hinges. They pushed it and went in.

It was immediately obvious as they entered that others had recently occupied their home. An overwhelming smell of decay and filth filled the air and was traced to an overflowing toilet, which had frozen over the winter, but had continued to be used. Discarded pieces of tattered clothing lay around; the floor was dotted with used contraceptives and unidentified stains. A fire had burned in the centre of the sitting room floor, fuelled by smashed furniture. But there was still limited running water and electricity in the kitchen and the laundry room. Cooking pots were found discarded in a corner and the large brown leather kitchen sofa was vigorously cleaned to provide a bed for Berta.

From the yard and outhouses Erhard gathered wood and coal to fuel the stove, undamaged but filthy. In the first days after their return they boiled water to clean and scrub, unblocked the toilet, shovelled up heaps of refuse and excrement, attempted to board up broken windows and doors for security, and tried to erase the stench and grime, all without gloves. Valuable rugs had been thrown onto a nearby dung heap and could not be rescued.

A picture of events during their absence was pieced together from the evidence in the house and comments by neighbours. The house had been set up as a brothel by American troops, and whether the local girls were coerced or acted willingly depended on which version was believed. To returning refugees such as Minny, local events and developments were of greater immediate relevance than any wider political situation.

They learned that the two flanks of the pincer-like "circle", which American forces had closed around Aachen, had finally met in the area near Kaisersruh on 16th October of the previous year, and the nearby villages of Würselen and Haaren had witnessed intense combat in the final weeks before hostilities ceased on 21st October.

The "Battle for Crucifix Hill", on the outskirts of Haaren, would become a byword for the last desperate stand and the names of American Army divisions which took credit for closing the circle around the city entered Aachen history: Roosevelt's Butchers (*Roosevelts Schlächter*) and the "Big Red One" after the red number "one" insignia of the unit. Hitler's dream of a new thousand-year Reich emanating from the imperial city had come to a bloody and dreadful end in the vicinity of their home.

Bomb-damaged Ursulinerstrasse, Aachen

Aachen and Environs 1944
(Selected Detail)

NETHERLANDS

Würselen

Kaisersruh

GERMANY

West Wall

Haaren

(To Stolberg)

Vaals
(NL)

Vaalserquartier
(Germany)

AACHEN

BELGIUM

(To Eupen)

| 0 Miles | 1 | 2 | | - - - - | Country Borders |
| 0 KM | 1 | 2 | 3 | —— | Roads |

An official transfer from American command of Aachen to the British Military Government under Lt. Col. G.F. Parrott of 1011 Detachment was not completed until 23rd June, so American troops were still much in evidence in the period of chaos and transition, as Minny, Berta and Erhard rescued what they could of home and possessions. Soldiers came silently to the house at dusk, in large leather boots, looking for girls. Minny hid in the kitchen cupboard or under the stairs until she heard their retreating footsteps. Venturing out to farms, she observed familiar linen and rugs in use. The farmers' families denied knowledge of how household items from Kaisersruh had come into their possession, muttering excuses of "for safekeeping", and grudgingly returned some at Minny's request. Prisoners released from camps had looted any remaining clothes found in the house, wearing them as they continued to work as farm hands.

Lawlessness forced everyone to look out for themselves. Although the Allied zones had officially already been created, the Allied Control Council, which was to govern the four zones into which Germany was divided, did not first meet in Berlin until 30th July (see Historical Note 4).

There were rumours that many who had stayed in their houses had profited from the misfortunes of others, and had "appropriated" what could be salvaged before the rightful owners returned. A joke circulated that some farms had "carpets in the pigsty". A pun was made on the German verb *sicherstellen* – to take possession of or confiscate – where the second part of the verb (*-stellen*) was changed to *stehlen* – to steal. One of the Nellessens' elderly gardeners had refused to be evacuated with his family and been forcibly taken to nearby barracks where hundreds were still temporarily housed, but not before he had engaged in "securing" items from the estate.

Erhard cleared refuse in the garden, excavating hiding places where valuables had been dug in, but most had either been blown to pieces or already unearthed and looted. Some kitchen porcelain, however, had survived, protected in large zinc tubs. The question uppermost in everyone's mind was all too familiar: what could be found to eat?

A few shrivelled vegetables were still in the ground. Milk was available from the farms, distributed in milk churns, and ration coupons could be exchanged in Würselen, where, in spite of widespread destruction, temporary kitchens had been set up for hundreds of returning refugees. Even after the fall of Aachen, Würselen had been fiercely fought over as German resistance tried to break the ring around the city and Allied troops attempted to secure their gains in their push inland towards the Rhine. Minny cycled up the hill with empty pans to be filled with soup or stew.

Tentatively investigating the main estate house where the Nellessens had lived, Minny's family found it in better shape than their own. Windows were shattered, furniture was piled up in heaps as barricades, and much of the cellar was under water, but it was structurally sound. Erhard found a bed frame to sleep on. Part of the cellar wall behind which Herr Nellessen had sealed in his collection of watches and clocks had been broken open; his treasures were gone. They were later told that an American military detachment had operated from there in the weeks before the fall of the city in mid-October.

Late one evening in the last week of May, in driving rain, they heard the roar of a motorcycle engine and noises of movement coming from the main house. They wisely did not investigate, apprehensive of unknown new developments. Over the following days they observed groups of soldiers moving in with equipment, wearing unfamiliar uniforms. This was a British advance party for 64 Field Security Section, part of the Intelligence Corps, who now appropriated Kaisersruh in support of their local operations.

A unit of about 15 British officers and soldiers were responsible for monitoring and surveying a stretch of the border between Germany and Holland, establishing stability and security, and in particular screening individuals who might be senior Nazis fleeing Germany.

They were to work in close collaboration with the Dutch border authorities and be based nearby at the frontier with the Netherlands. Planning for the control of occupied Germany's borders after her defeat had already been put in place in early 1944 (see Historical Note 5).

Proximity ensured that the new occupants of Kaisersruh quickly became aware of their neighbours, as the two houses were just yards apart. In brief initial formal contact, Minny, Berta and Erhard encountered British soldiers face-to-face for the first time, burdened with preconceptions about "the other side" formed through the baggage of two world conflicts.

The British were better prepared, however, since some in the unit had experience of Germany before the war. In addition, as representatives of the Empire, they had been issued with detailed written guidelines on correct behaviour and attitudes, and were briefed on the German character. "Instructions for British Servicemen in Germany 1944" stated:

> *"When you meet the Germans you will probably think they are very much like us. They look like us, except that there are fewer of the wiry type and more big, fleshy, fair-haired men and women, especially in the north. But they are not really so much like us as they look. The Germans have of course many good qualities. They are very hard-working and thorough; they are obedient and have a great love of tidiness and order."*

One evening, a persistent knock at the Rösslers' door forced Minny to open cautiously. *"Könnten Sie uns bitte Tee kochen, Fräulein?"*, asked a slim soldier in British uniform, with dark-rimmed glasses – "could you please make us some tea?" Although some members of the unit had already moved into the main house, sleeping in rows on the floor of the hall, as yet no cooking facilities existed. Minny boiled water for a small amount of pre-prepared tea granules, combined with sugar and milk powder, and he returned to his quarters. Neither had any inkling that they had just met their future spouse.

Jim McCormack, 1945

The next day the same soldier was once again at the door with a proposition expressed in faultless "high" German. The intelligence unit of officers and other ranks would be working from headquarters established a few kilometres away in the former *Zollhaus* – customs house – in the suburb of Vaalserquartier on the Dutch border, but they intended to use the Nellessens' house as a Mess and for additional sleeping quarters. Another controlled crossing point was set up at Herzogenrath, a few kilometres away. Minny and her family, he explained, might remain in their house on condition of agreeing to act as housekeepers: cooking, washing and serving meals. Payment would be in the army rations which formed the basis of their meals. The offer of a ready supply of rations which did not have to be sought out and bartered ensured a swift "yes" in response.

The British Army Captain commanding the unit, Clifford Pennison, had set up his office in Herr Nellessen's gun room on the first floor, which overlooked the Rössler house. With experience of working in Berlin before the war, he now conducted searching interviews in German with Minny, Berta and Erhard in which they explained their family background and gave accounts of movements and activities during the years of war; answers were noted down in official paperwork. Eventually the written *Fragebogen* (questionnaire) would be in place, an instrument in the policy of political and social re-education, or *Entnazifizierung* (denazification), already deliberated by representatives of the Allied nations well before a formal end to hostilities, but not yet practically implemented. Citizens wishing to be considered for employment in a public sphere would be categorized according to their degree of involvement in the former regime (see Historical Note 6). Theoretically, anyone with status above that of labourer was to give account of their activities.

But the Rössler family interviews leading to their employment by the British took place just days after the official establishment of the zones through the "Berlin Declaration" of 5th June. In the interests of setting in motion both the unit's work at the frontier and the family's employment in support of its smooth running, as swiftly as possible, it is unlikely they ever received any "official" categorization, as they were merely being screened for domestic work. But Minny's involvement with the BDM, wartime employment at the Aachen Police station and nominal membership of the NSDAP inevitably led to particularly probing questioning. Erhard had been a member of the Hitler Youth and served in the *Wehrmacht*. Berta had not been an NSDAP member and was interviewed in the kitchen where she was at work, as a courtesy by Captain Pennison, who applied for corroboration of everyone's details in Würselen, the town in whose administrative district they lived. Minny's NSDAP membership record states Würselen as her local party group. He was evidently satisfied with the results of his enquiries, for official permits were eventually issued, stating that Minny, Berta and Erhard were employed by the British. They set to work.

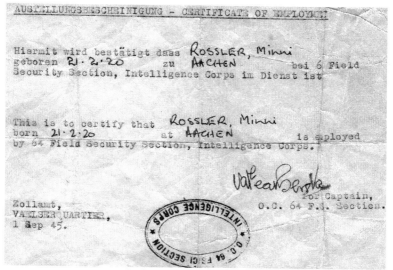

Minny's work permit

Initially meals were prepared in the kitchen of the smaller stone house, and carried over to the larger Kaisersruh quarters, until its own ground floor kitchen was cleaned and the stove coaxed into life with wood and coal salvaged from the cellar. Representatives from the new British occupants of the estate paid the Nellessens a courtesy visit, explaining developments in their erstwhile home. From their temporary quarters with Frau Nellessen's sister in Laurensberg, a suburb of Aachen a few kilometres away, Herr Nellessen generously offered to bring the former furnishings out of storage on the strict understanding that their hiding place was not revealed, and that they would be returned after the unit's departure.

Huge trucks crawled up the drive to the main house at Kaisersruh and unloaded American and British army rations, which were stacked in a storage room next to the kitchen, and locked. As Berta and Minny demonstrated reliability and honesty, Berta was entrusted with the keys. She proved to be an excellent housekeeper, demanding high standards from her staff, whose work she sternly inspected, wearing white gloves which she wiped over surfaces to check their cleanliness. Girls were hired from Würselen to help make beds, prepare food, wash up and clean. They too were screened. Minny served food, which was hoisted to the first floor dining room from the kitchen in a small lift, and cleared the table, wearing a starched protective white apron and her hair pinned up.

Berta's creativity was stretched to the limit devising meals from often unfamiliar ingredients. Fresh dairy produce came from the adjacent farms, but was supplemented with dried egg and milk powder. The farmers exchanged fresh meat, predominantly beef, for commodities, as the local economy was still largely based on barter. Huge unsweetened white loaves were delivered daily, a new experience as they were used to dark rye and wholegrain breads. But a large proportion of food arrived sealed in large drums and tins.

They had never before tasted peanut butter, baked beans in tomato sauce, spam or corned beef. Berta concocted a kind of corned beef hash, with tinned tomatoes, fried onions and sliced potatoes. Breakfast consisted of a brew made from a ready-mixed powder of tea, milk and sugar, with scrambled eggs, also from powder, eaten with bacon, and bread spread with pineapple jam, from large tins. Even desserts appeared on the menu, largely based on fresh, powdered or condensed milk, as well as baked flans and cakes. Berta was in constant pain, as the wound on her right hand, where the thumb had been amputated, was not fully healed. Even before the amputation it was inflexible and often painful, resulting from sinews damaged when, as a young girl, she had crashed into a window while skating outside.

Duty started at 6am, seven days a week. Washing was initially done by hand in the yard, until Berta began to contract out washing to women from Würselen, who collected and returned it, receiving food rations as payment. Gradually Kaisersruh was cleaned and made habitable, and all the upstairs bedrooms brought back into use. Berta acquired considerable standing in the neighbourhood by providing desperately needed employment for local people, recently returned from the front or after evacuation, in a fragile economy just starting to gain momentum. Word spread of their access to food supplies and acquaintances from before the war turned up at the house seeking handouts. Minny admits to hiding a former school classmate in a store room and supplying sandwiches without anyone's knowledge. New rulings and directives issued by the Military Government were attached as notices in both languages to walls and doors.

The acquisition of new glass for the shattered windows illustrated the slowly reviving collaborative post-war economy. The British issued a Dutch glass manufacturer permits to dig sand from his sand pits in Germany, provided he supplied glass for Kaisersruh. The recently re-appointed *Bürgermeister* (mayor) of the local town of Würselen arranged the glazing and cleaning, receiving in return surplus glass for refurbishment in the town. While Kaisersruh was by no means fully returned to its former state, accommodation and messing facilities now enjoyed by the unit were far superior to that of others in the area! Silk carpets were re-laid, curtains and floral wall hangings re-hung, elegant antique French Rococo dining chairs upholstered in costly fabrics once again flanked the dining table. Herr Nellessen's smoking room, hung with hunting trophies, became a sitting room for the house's temporary occupants. There was even a grand piano. The small unit of officers and soldiers "messed" together in one dining room, with everyone eating identical meals at one table.

The British at Kaisersruh initially conducted day-to-day business in an efficient and distant manner, as "official" policy dictated. Each day Berta and Minny received instructions in German from Jim, the soldier who had first requested tea. On leave when the property was first appropriated, he had joined the unit from headquarters in Brussels. With a fluent command of German, French and Dutch, he also interpreted for Minny, Berta and Erhard, and was engaged in screening and interviewing the thousands of Displaced Persons (DPs), predominantly from Slavic and eastern European states, at Vaalserquartier, who wished to cross the border and return to homes and families. DPs came to gain a reputation for lawlessness and violence, and many were prosecuted and punished by British justice. In addition, the unit continued to search for fleeing Nazis. At this point, German nationals were not permitted to leave the country, and many higher NSDAP officials in an automatic arrest category attempted to do so to avoid detection.

Field Security personnel were selected for their language skills. Jim and his colleagues held screening interviews in German, as a person's true identity might be unwittingly revealed by discrepancies and nuances of language and accent, as well as by examination of personal effects. One young woman held for interview claimed to be of Dutch origin, but further questioning and investigation of scant possessions revealed an SS tattoo, and photographs with soldiers wearing SS insignia.

Beyond the necessary formalities, the British were expected not to "fraternise", a policy established as early as September 1944 by the Allied Command. The "Instructions to British Servicemen" books issued to troops serving in Germany explained German history and culture. Above all, it warned against developing sympathy for the Germans, representatives of the "vanquished" nation:

> "You will see much suffering in Germany and much to awake your pity. You may also find that many Germans, on the surface at least, seem pleasant enough and that they will even try to welcome you as friends. All this may make you think that they have learned their lesson and need no further teaching. But remember this: for the last hundred years – long before Hitler – German writers of great authority have been steadily teaching the necessity for war and glorifying it for its own sake. At least the Germans have much to unlearn. They have also much to atone for"

In March 1945, as troops stood poised by the Rhine, Montgomery had emphasised the ban on fraternisation in a "Letter by the Commander-in-Chief on Non-Fraternisation". But shortly after the total capitulation of 8th May, Montgomery's attitude was already more conciliatory, and on 12th

154 · INGRID DIXON

June it was announced the ban was no longer to apply to "small children". By July he maintained: "our present attitude towards the German people is negative, it must be replaced by one that is positive and holds out hope for the future". Another letter was issued on 14th July, relaxing the ban further: troops were permitted to enter into "conversation with adult Germans in the streets and in public places" but not in their homes. At Kaisersruh this boundary had already been crossed.

In Britain, a lively discussion was triggered in the press. Non-fraternisation principles ultimately proved to be unrealistic and unworkable in the reality of most day-to-day situations. Debates were conducted in the wider context of trying to answer a fundamental question: what should the Allies be trying to achieve? Were they in Germany merely as conquerors, establishing moral superiority? Or should they be attempting to help the German nation back on to its feet, to give it hope for the future? The latter viewpoint was eventually to gain dominance, underpinned by the implementation of both the Marshall Plan and the Berlin Airlift, and the rejection of the so-called Morgenthau plan, which sought to dismantle German industry and reduce her to an agrarian economy, unable to regain a credible profile in Europe. A new threat was also being recognised and discussed by both politicians in Britain and those governing in Germany: a German population brought to its knees by hunger, malnutrition and humiliation was more susceptible to the growing threat of Communism, against which an economically stronger Germany might act as a bulwark. Many in Britain were shocked by the vigour with which Montgomery, his deputies and successors turned their efforts almost overnight to the rebuilding and regeneration of Germany, and in particular to preventing widespread starvation.

Some weeks after they had started working for the British, at the beginning of August 1945, Minny was serving lunch, the main meal of the day, when she was asked to leave the dining room to go outside. Her father, Emil, had been found lying at the end of the drive, unable to move in a state of exhausted collapse after a lengthy and tortuous journey home. As he was helped into the house, he was briefed on the new arrangements with which he would be confronted. His family, up to that moment, had had no knowledge of whether he had survived. He had been held in a British prisoner-of-war camp in Eutin, in Northern Germany, where conditions of overcrowding were so severe that there was no adequate shelter and only meagre food. Prisoners squatted in the open in a quagmire, linking arms to prevent each other sinking into the mud.

Over the next weeks he related his experiences and began to regain strength, aided by medicines and food provided by the British military, whose compatriots a few weeks previously had been his captors. Like Erhard, he had slowly made his way home through destroyed towns and ravaged countryside by begging for transport on military vehicles from both sides, resting in fields at night and scavenging food where he could.

Captain Pennison demonstrated compassion in ensuring Emil received adequate rations and medication, even though he was not in British employ. The unit commander, in common with others in the occupation forces, was confronted on a daily basis with effecting a mental transition from the destruction of a country and its people to contributing to its rebuilding and regeneration. Attitudes and behaviour of individuals were governed by random factors such as age, background and war experiences. Those with a Jewish background, or present when concentration camps were liberated, confronted the issues with a distinct set of emotions.

One morning as Minny entered the Kaisersruh house and prepared to start work, she noticed German words scrawled on the white kitchen door: "Darling Minny" ran the gist, "when will you be mine?", and ostensibly signed by Jim. How should she react? It could not be ignored in the proximity of daily working contact. Jim later broached the subject himself and admitted rather sheepishly that the words were the product of an over-indulgence of alcohol the previous evening. It is likely that his companions had written the declaration as a joke or dare!

But some weeks later Jim, during a snatched moment alone with Minny, risked another comment. She was unsure how to interpret it. Attraction was present on both sides, as yet unacknowledged and suppressed but quietly observed by family and colleagues. It is interesting to speculate whether Jim was cautioned against pursuing the relationship at this point, either by his commander or fellow soldiers.

By August 1945, the singular circumstances at Kaisersruh had come to the attention of superiors, representatives of Colonel Parrott's Military Government detachment overseeing Aachen. 64 FSS had moved into Kaisersruh several weeks in advance of the British taking over control of the city, and is not mentioned by name in the Colonel's war diary entries for June 1945.

In contrast to other locations in the British-occupied zone, where conquerors and conquered predominantly lived, worked and spent leisure time in strict separation, boundaries at Kaisersruh were more fluid, enabled by their location outside the city, coupled with a certain autonomy enjoyed by Field Security units. Officially under the auspices of the Military Government, their role was nevertheless distinct in the peculiar circumstances of the post-war order.

The house at Kaisersruh was taken over by the Military Government and 64 FSS had to move. It has to be assumed that Parrott or a deputy initiated the change. Eventually representatives of the Belgian military moved into the building, but not before, as promised, the Nellessen's costly furnishings were taken back into storage. Herr Nellessen, who was reassured on learning that Minny and her family were in the employment of the British on his estate, never inspected the new arrangements himself; he was forced to monitor its fate at a distance, having sustained an injury after a fall down cellar stairs.

New premises and sleeping quarters – a villa owned by the Goldhausen family, who owned a lighting and lamp business in Aachen – were found directly adjacent to the existing headquarters in Vaalserquartier, which continued to function as before. The owners had no choice but to accept the temporary requisitioning and moved away. Policies on requisitioning houses for occupying forces and their families, in operation in the British Zone as a whole, gave rise to widespread deep resentment, reinforcing the notion of an insensitive and even hostile occupier. Many German citizens forced to relinquish properties were not compensated in kind as the Rössler family were being recompensed for their labours. In subsequent years of the British occupation, controversy would emerge over the "acquisition" of antiques and valuables by members of the Control Commission and the military government.

Minny, Berta and Erhard had become an essential element in the smooth running of domestic arrangements. Erhard had felt empathy with the British from the outset. He ran errands, cleaned and helped to service motorcycles and military trucks marked with a white star, a symbol common to most Allied vehicles, and was on hand to unload supplies of rations, in collaboration with two older German employees, who had been "adopted" by the unit on account of their useful skills and maintained the Jeeps and trucks in good running order. Erhard recalls having to paint new insignia on military vehicles requisitioned by the British: a spearhead mounted in a diamond shape.

Negotiations initiated by Captain Pennison led to the family being re-housed in Vaalserquartier, so that their employment, beneficial to both parties, could continue. Scant possessions and a small amount of furniture were transported from Kaisersruh to Gut Klau, a large rambling farmhouse where several families were housed on different floors. Bedding and clothes were wrapped around remaining china and cooking utensils, and placed in the trunk, once more loaded onto a truck for the short journey of a few kilometres. The Rössler family never returned to their former home. In compensation for their loss, Herr Nellessen gifted them a plot of land before he died, which they eventually sold, using the proceeds to buy a house for retirement in Haaren.

In the Goldhausen family villa, Minny and Berta adapted to cooking in new surroundings. Previously, the unit's administrative base had been separated from its sleeping and messing premises at Kaisersruh by several kilometres. Now Minny established a routine of crossing the few yards over the street from their kitchens to the offices where Jim was at work, delivering teapots with freshly brewed tea at strategic points of the day, and waving to the Dutch official manning the border barrier for crossing into Holland. Soon after the move, Minny recalls the news of the Japanese surrender echoing around the building. 15th August 1945. War on all fronts was finally over.

In the weeks since the take-over of Kaisersruh, occupiers and occupied had developed formal but friendly relations. Underpinned by centuries of colonial history in contact with "vanquished" peoples, the British ran the unit with practiced ease. Most of the motley crew of officers and soldiers were anxious to return to Britain, to civilian occupations held before the outbreak of war. Jim continued to observe Minny as she served meals with good humour and efficiency, and in private dared to imagine a future with her. But he was aware of the constraints, even though concessions to the realities of the situation had been recognised. As "Instructions for British Servicemen" said:

> "Germany will not be a pleasant place to live in after the war, and German girls know that, if they marry, they will become British with all the advantages of belonging to a victor nation instead of to a vanquished one. Many German girls will be just waiting for the chance to marry a Briton – whether they care for him or not. When once they had their marriage lines he would have served his purpose."

Never comfortable in a military environment, and always distrustful of military authority, Jim had confided in colleague Paul Butcher, but admitted he would never risk discipline by openly fraternising beyond what was considered acceptable. Others continued to bait him mercilessly.

The ban on "fraternisation with the enemy" was finally relaxed by Montgomery on 25th September, in a message to all members of British forces in Germany, with the exception that no Allied soldiers were to be billeted with Germans or be allowed to inter-marry. The announcement was celebrated with a party organised at Vaalserquartier. Jim now felt he might risk expressing his feelings for Minny more publicly. Unofficially, many others in the unit had already started forming liaisons with local girls, which were quietly sanctioned by their superiors. Marriage with the former enemy, the ultimate form of reconciliation, was still banned.

TO ALL MEMBERS OF THE
BRITISH FORCES IN GERMANY

1. The Allied Control Council has decided
that the time has come to abolish all
separate zonal orders on the subject of non-
fraternisation with the German people,
and to adopt a universal policy which will
ensure uniform treatment of Germany.

2. All present orders about non-fraternisation are now cancelled.

3. The following orders will remain in force:-

   (a) No members of the armed forces will
   be billeted with German families.

   (b) Members of the armed forces will
   not be permitted to marry Germans.

4. I rely on all members of the armed forces
to conduct themselves with dignity, and to use
their common sense, when dealing with the
Germans: twice our enemies in war during
the last 30 years.

B. L. Montgomery
Field Marshal,
Commander-in-Chief,
25 Sep 45   British Army of the Rhine.

Opportunities to be alone were limited. Jim and Minny took walks in the tranquil woods and fields near their accommodation at Vaalserquartier, offering privacy and quiet. In pre-war days and even later, Minny had been closely chaperoned by her parents. Now, aged 25, she could finally express herself freely. What did they discuss? Jim, in his faultless German, told Minny tales of his childhood, of his family, people she had never met in a country she had never visited. It is not hard to imagine the directions their conversations must have taken: the unique circumstances which had led to their meeting, German preconceptions about the British and *vice-versa,* and the respective leaders of the two nations. Jim was full of admiration for Churchill but talked of Montgomery with disdain. Ironically, Montgomery – like Jim – had come to develop sympathy for the German people. Although constrained by obligations not to breach confidentiality, and with an exaggerated fear of discipline, Jim may have explained some of the more mundane aspects of his daytime work at Vaalserquartier. German nationals he interviewed at the border frequently attempted to play down or conceal involvement with the previous regime. A much repeated phrase in the post-war months was *"ich war immer dagegen"* – "I was always against them" – as individuals re-wrote personal histories. Jim received "gifts" of incriminating books printed during the Third Reich, from those seeking to discard evidence of political sympathies.

He is unlikely to have described to Minny his memories of living as a civilian in London during the Blitz, before being called up in 1940, or coming under V2 rocket attack when stationed in Antwerp in late 1944. These events may have been too raw in experience to address. In typical British understatement, his mother Nora had written to an Irish relative in September 1940 that Jim "had a very nasty time" in London. Nor would he have shared with her details of moving with his unit into Germany in late Spring 1945. They might, though, have talked of former relationships.

Minny recalls that she was drawn by Jim's honesty and integrity, by his down-to-earth humanity and generous nature, even in the ambiguous post-war circumstances. "I was first attracted by his eyes", she confesses and by the fact that "I never really felt he was an *Ausländer* (foreigner) or a former adversary". When on duty, he invariably managed a pleasant remark, negotiating a difficult path between the formality and awkwardness of fraternisation policies and a desire to appear human.

These qualities are borne out by surviving Army records, where superiors comment on Jim's "exemplary" conduct and bearing. But he could also appear uneasy in social situations, and did not readily form close friendships. Jim was analytical, enjoyed arguing a point and hated spectator sports, in contrast to Minny, who had an easy-going, conciliatory and forgiving nature and had frequently attended local football matches in her teens. Like many young Britons of his generation, Jim had had left-wing sympathies in the 1930s. When refugees from the

Spanish civil war arrived in Liverpool and were temporarily housed nearby, Jim, ever eager for more linguistic practice, used to meet them to discuss politics in Spanish.

Jim and Minny even went out with other couples in similar situations, in spite of continuing curfews and restrictions. Paul had met Marianne, a German girl from Herzogenrath, the border suburb where the unit also ran an outpost. German women, present in far greater numbers than men, were eager to make social contact with the British. Together the four drove out in an army Jeep. Jim had never learned to drive, so Paul took the wheel. On a country track, he had to swerve to avoid an oncoming vehicle, leaving the roadside briefly. As he set off again, a large mine exploded behind them, which they must have disturbed. They thought the whole incident comical.

One excursion took them into the Hürtgen Forest, where large parts were still cordoned off as no-go areas, and a terrible stench of death pervaded. Jim had read about the slaughter and was curious to see the terrain for himself.

Berta and Emil observed the relationship developing and can only too easily have imagined and dreaded a possible future scenario. Their family bonds were close, deepened by shared experiences of war-time hardships. It was hard to contemplate a future without their daughter's presence.

One evening in December Jim and Minny walked over to Gut Klau and told Berta and Emil they planned one day to marry. Emil located one cracked schnapps glass, which had to be passed from person to person, to toast the couple. But how must they have reacted in private? They had no personal animosity against Jim, as they had observed him for many months. But they cannot have welcomed the news with enthusiasm either.

The first Christmas of peace passed. An uncertain future lay ahead.

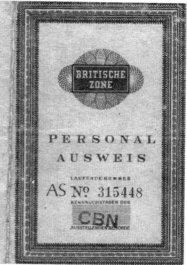

Minny's identification card in the British occupation zone

Within the image:

Zur Beachtung!

1. Der Inhaber hat diesen Ausweis jederzeit bei sich zu tragen und auf Verlangen alliierter oder deutscher Dienststellen und ihrer Beauftragten sowie sonstiger dazu berechtigter Personen vorzuzeigen.

2. Der Inhaber ist für diesen Ausweis verantwortlich und darf ihn niemand anderem überlassen. Verlust, Vernichtung, Beschädigung oder Unkenntlichwerden des Ausweises ist umgehend der zuständigen Meldebehörde anzuzeigen.

3. Wer einen verlorenen Ausweis findet oder einen Ausweis besitzt, der nicht ihm selbst oder einer seiner Obhut unterstehenden Person gehört, hat ihn bei einer Meldebehörde oder einer Polizeibehörde abzuliefern.

4. Jeder Verstoss gegen diese Vorschriften ist strafbar.

BRITISCHE ZONE

PERSONAL AUSWEIS

LAUFENDE NUMMER
AS № 315448
KENNBUCHSTABEN DER

CBN
AUSSTELLENDEN BEHÖRDE

CHAPTER EIGHT

1946: Separation

If Emil and Bertha had doubts about the wisdom of Minny's decision to get engaged they didn't voice them. Although Minny learned later that Jim's family expressed dismay at the announcement, a steady flow of letters began to arrive from James and Honora McCormack, always known as Jim and Nora, her future parents-in-law.

Letter from Liverpool, opened and re-sealed by censors

As a self-taught and professional linguist, Jim McCormack senior responded to the news with encouraging letters in faultless and elegant German. Both Nora and Jim's younger sister, Thea, wrote in English, which Jim translated for Minny. The first letter Nora wrote, dated February 1946, was kind and welcoming. The misgivings felt on learning of her eldest son's engagement to "one of the enemy" are not even hinted at.

To mark the engagement, Emil took a heavy gold ring engraved with his initials to a jeweller in Aachen and had a piece removed to form a gold band for Minny. In Germany, an engagement ring functions as a wedding ring too. During the engagement period it is worn on the left hand, and transferred to the right hand on marriage. The original ring, made of Turkish gold, had been bought by Emil in Istanbul when he had been seconded to the Turkish Army during the First World War, instructing Turkish infantry troops in German military tactics. For this he had been awarded an inscribed Turkish service medal and formal certificate of thanks in Ottoman Turkish script.

By March of that year Jim had received his "demob" (demobilisation) orders, and prepared to return to England. Feelings of anticipation at a reunion with his family were mixed with regret at leaving. Conversations in the weeks before departure were dominated by the future. As the law still forbade British soldiers from marrying German women, there was no precedent to follow, no set path or accepted way of proceeding, as a new post-war society was emerging in both countries. Even supposing British law would eventually sanction such unions, how would the necessary permits and documents for Minny to reach Britain be obtained? Obstacles not even anticipated would stand in the way. Where or when they would meet again was uncertain. But both could be thankful that they had survived the war without loss of parents or siblings.

Jim left for England at the end of April 1946, optimistic, hopeful and reassured that the Rössler family in Germany would receive ongoing food rations by continuing to work for 64 FSS. His certificate of transfer to the Army reserve, marking the end of the period as a serving soldier, is dated 10th May 1946.

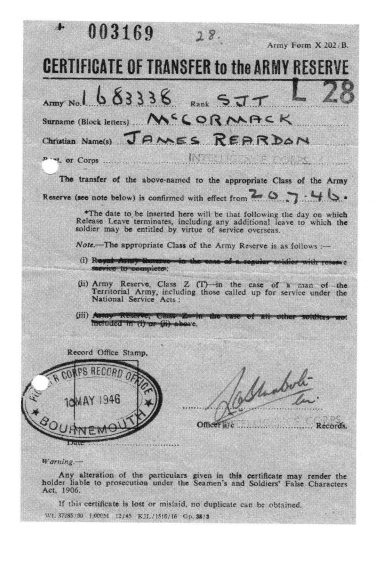

The reunion with his family is described by his father, Jim senior, in fluent German in a letter to Minny dated 13th May, which he signs *Vati und Mutti* – Mum and Dad:

> *"Jim arrived home safely but weary and in good spirits. Of course many of our conversations centre around you!" he writes, "and your parents and brother. Since Tony [Jim's brother, waiting to be demobilised from the RAF] is able to spend time at home at present, the two brothers are often out and about, and in the evenings the five of us chat, just like in the old days before the war. Dear Mother positively beams at having her 3 children together again! I'm sure you will get on with her, Minny!"*

Did they privately hope the relationship would not weather both time spent apart and obstacles which stood in the couples' way? In their son they recognised determination and commitment. Having once set his mind on a goal, he would pursue it patiently by all possible means.

In Germany, a new order was emerging from the wasteland of the "Zero Hour" of May 1945, determined by Allied policies and fraught with controversy and complexity (see Historical Note 7). British junior Minister John Hynd, as representative of Clement Attlee's newly elected Labour government, had been appointed as overall governor of the British "element" of the Allied post-war administrations on 22nd October 1945 and regularly briefed the British government on the realities of the tasks it faced. In particular, denazification, and the internment of those suspected of involvement with the former regime while evidence was being established, were the focus of ongoing agonising, as British politicians and occupiers alike increasingly came to view denazification policies as being at odds with a more constructive concept of "re-education". Responsibility for concluding the lengthy denazification investigations were systematically handed over to newly established German civilian bodies and would be concluded by 1948.

As Minny made enquiries about former colleagues from the police station, she discovered that many had not returned from the war. Law, order and the restructuring and training of a post-war police force was conducted in Aachen under the jurisdiction of Colonel Parrott, the British Military Government commander. For the Zone as a whole, a police school had been set up, re-training and re-educating those who had been screened and wished to be considered for re-employment. By August 1945, the pre-war *Polizeipräsidium* – police station – where Minny had worked, was once more usable. She learned that some colleagues classified in lower categories of involvement with the regime were carrying out community service in Aachen, or had had fines imposed. One was in charge of a *Trümmerkommando* – a squad of people clearing rubble. Minny continued to receive a salary from the state until May 1945 and in later years was entitled to claim a pension.

Building rubble, Germany 1945

Aachen had experienced a head start of just under seven months of occupation, compared with the rest of the British Zone. The American military garrison established at the end of October 1944 had already started surveying the destroyed urban landscape and carrying out a tentative amount of rebuilding and reconstruction, severely hampered by lack of craftsmen and available manpower and materials.

After the hand-over to the British, a new body of town councillors had been proposed and elected in November 1945. Now, political party activity could resume and trade unions be refounded, under British supervision. The British Military Government papers on Aachen from 1945 and 1946 document steady, perceptible progress in the re-establishment of law and order, water and sewerage supplies, public health, education, transport, business and commerce; rubble was cleared, roads repaired, schools re-opened. But the straightforward, neutral, narrative language of the monthly reports only hints at the continuing crises in fuel, housing and infrastructure and masks the tragedies of thousands of individual lives, many of which resulted directly from Allied policies.

A Field Security unit was also operating in the city of Aachen, in addition to Jim's unit at the border. Field Security units in other areas of occupied Germany were responsible for arresting von Ribbentrop, who had been Hitler's ambassador to Britain before the war, and Nicholas von Below, Hitler's adjutant, who was allegedly the last person to see Hitler alive and was a signatory to his will. The fear of widespread "Werewolf"–type resistance, however, had proved to be groundless.

Much painstaking planning undertaken prior to unconditional surrender had had to be revised on a daily basis in the light of actual circumstances "on the ground". It had quickly become apparent, for instance, that policies on movements around border areas, and in particular those preventing German citizens crossing frontiers, were unworkable. Children became the "ice-breakers", asking for handouts of a *Butterbrot* – sandwich – from the border guards and dodging frontier controls to slip back and forth. Officials on both sides turned a blind eye. Returning civilians wished to visit relatives and parties of local residents holding social gatherings, across the barbed-wire fences at the Vaalser-quartier and Herzogenrath crossing points, could frequently be observed. The death of a young German woman shot by a panicking Dutch official led Paul Butcher at 64 FSS to initiate a scheme for cross-border visiting permits to be issued, which was authorised by his Army superiors.

While a physical environment could be gradually reconstructed, mental damage, trauma and personal guilt and responsibility had to be dealt with individually. Both Protestant and Catholic churches reflected on their roles under the National Socialist regime. The Council of Evangelical Churches had issued the "Stuttgart Declaration" in the autumn of 1945, acknowledging guilt in not opposing the regime with enough vehemence. For Germans, no counselling centres existed to assist with grieving, loss and healing; at that time, there was little talk of such things. Daily physical survival in the face of devastating food and fuel shortages was still the overwhelming priority for the majority.

British press reports of ongoing hardships prevalent in Germany met with mixed responses. In March, a film-maker, Humphrey Jennings, had first screened his film "A Defeated People" in London, documenting the realities of conditions in Germany. Many in Britain were understandably un-sympathetic, feeling the German population was paying a just price for what their leaders had unleashed on the world, brought into grim focus as concentration camps had been liberated and photographs published. There was also publically expressed resentment at the astronomical and growing cost of contributing to the reconstruction of Germany.

In spite of penalties for those caught dealing and buying, a black market still flourished in Germany. Profiteering and corruption were endemic on both sides. Much surviving paperwork still in existence from the frontier crossing point at the German/Dutch border at Vaalserquartier, code-named "Whip", where Jim had worked, relates to smuggling of goods and those engaged in illicit trafficking. The Reichsmark would not be replaced until a currency reform of 1948. Skills of bartering honed in the war continued to be essential tools for living.

The most valued currency was cigarettes, issued to British servicemen and forming a portion of the payment in kind received by Minny and her family. Cigarettes were supplied in small round metal tins, a pasted paper label advertising the brand. Berta, ever thrifty, kept some for decades as button tins.

Emil had recovered sufficiently from incarceration in a British prisoner-of-war camp to be able to join squads of men formed to clear mines and make the countryside safer. Hastily trained and inadequately equipped, he often returned home with tales of colleagues who had lost limbs or even their lives in the course of work.

Then word reached them that Doctor Kremer, the former family doctor from Haaren, was to re-open his practice. At that time doctors rarely drove themselves to visit patients, so Emil cycled daily to Haaren and worked as the doctor's chauffeur. While Minny continued to stand in queues or cycle to local farms and barter, a great deal of her time, efforts and thoughts were occupied with preparing for an eventual move to England, even though how or when this might happen was unclear.

She retrieved bed linen, sheets, pillow-cases and duvet covers embroidered with the family monogram, "v. K" (von Knappen) from Berta's brother Onkel Karl, who during the war had managed a large hotel in Wesel on the Lower Rhine, the Hotel Hof von Holland, and was now selling its assets and equipment to start a new venture. Wesel had been totally destroyed by Allied bombing in February and March 1945 as part of operations to advance to the Rhine, and had been occupied by British troops as early as March. Prior to its destruction, Karl had succeeded in transporting quantities of hotel goods to safety near Bremen. Erhard now travelled by goods train and collected items for his sister and parents.

Erhard's work for the British was supplemented by temporary jobs on local farms. He was eighteen, his schooling and adolescence disrupted by war. If he had any personal aspirations or hopes, they were overshadowed by efforts to stay alive.

Shortly after Jim's departure in May, Montgomery was replaced by Sholto Douglas as "Military Governor and Commander-in-Chief of all British Forces in Germany". On leaving Germany he issued "Notes on the German Situation" to Hynd, Attlee and the government, assessing achievements and progress, and outlining aims for the future. Where Montgomery was proud of accomplishments to date in the British Zone, regarding his tasks as a battle with moral and spiritual dimensions, Douglas would come to regard his tenure as one of the unhappiest periods in his life. The worsening food crisis would be blamed by many Germans on the policies of the Military Government.

As German nationals were still severely restricted in their movements, Minny applied for a travel pass in May, and in June took the train to visit her aunts in Heidelberg and Tante Lydia in Neckarsteinach, collecting the many items sent there for safekeeping. Berta was ready to help and give advice based on common preconceptions about the climate in Britain.

Old-fashioned fur stoles and hats which had belonged to Minny's grandmother joined the pile of items mounting up in the trunk "for England", a conventional bride's trousseau being assembled in unprecedented circumstances.

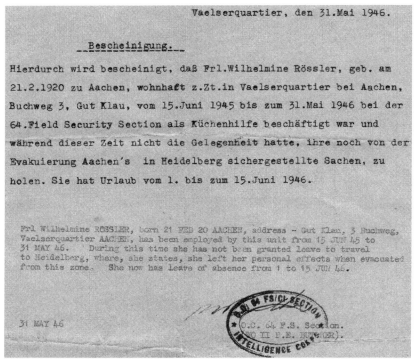

Pass permitting Minny to travel

During those months Minny was alternately worn down and encouraged by events. Encouragement came from the steady stream of uplifting letters from England from Jim and his family, describing life in Liverpool and the progress, or lack of it, being made for permission to leave Germany. All letters were numbered, to identify any that went astray. Most of those that reached her had been opened by censors. As soon as a letter with a British postmark arrived at their local post office, word spread like wildfire, and as direct delivery had not yet been re-established, it had to be collected. Jim had also arranged for parcels of groceries to be sent from Switzerland. But she was worn down by comments from neighbours in the vicinity, who had not been acquainted with Jim personally, and who wasted no time in expressing opinions on attachments to British men. *Den siehst du nie wieder,* (You'll never see him again) or *Soldatenliebchen* (soldier's sweetheart) were remarks frequently heard.

Extract from letter in Jim's handwriting about food shortages and food parcels sent via Switzerland

Jim's letters on his return to Britain are characterised by mundane descriptions of the civilian life to which he is adapting, interspersed with concern about ongoing privations in Germany featuring in the British press, and encouragement not to lose heart. To his future parents-in-law he expresses thanks for the way they have raised their daughter and for "the dearest, best life partner I ever could have wished to find in the whole world". He shares with Minny details of his savings and anticipated finances, prepares her for the reality of acute post-war housing shortages, which will hinder finding an eventual home, and describes a short holiday he has taken near Dartmouth in Devon, revelling once more in the English countryside. Expressions of longing for their eventual reunion permeate the correspondence.

He also wrote to other members of his former unit at the border, asking for confirmation of Minny's wellbeing. He had resumed working for the Civil Service in London, but attended lectures in the evenings, to pick up the threads of his disrupted education. A shortage of paper led to improvisation; Jim wrote lecture notes on the backs of used envelopes and recycled whatever could be found.

From August 1946 onwards, wives and families were able to join officer husbands in the British zone. Many experienced horror when confronted with the circumstances in post-war Germany, as German citizens rooted about in dustbins for food scraps and children begged constantly for a crust of bread. Yet more houses were requisitioned for accommodation, causing increased resentment. An exhibition "Germany under Control", opened by John Hynd in London in June, informing the population at home of conditions in the British Zone one year after total capitulation, attempted to document conditions in Germany.

While Minny had to ensure that paperwork was in place for eventual travel to England, Jim worked tirelessly and meticulously to establish the legal parameters in Britain. The breakthrough for many came in the summer of 1946 when the British Government relaxed the ban on servicemen being able to marry German nationals. In July and August, questions were asked in Parliament culminating in a statement on 1st

August that marriages with service personnel would be permitted.

Jim, though, was no longer serving, and, evidently confident of his status, had on 2nd July sent details of how she should proceed to secure the necessary permits. "The 21st July is not far off, the day when I am free to marry you" he wrote. This would be his first day as a civilian; he would no longer need permission to marry, but Minny would need authorisation from the British authorities to leave Germany and travel to Britain as his future wife.

"Write to the British Passport Control Officer at the British Consulate, Lübbecke", he wrote, "explain our circumstances, enclose my declaration [of intent to marry], and ask for permission to travel to England to marry me". He also gives details of how she should obtain permits for all the household goods she intends to take, applying to the Military Government in Aachen for an export permit. She would additionally have to apply for a transit visa through Holland, when everything else was in place.

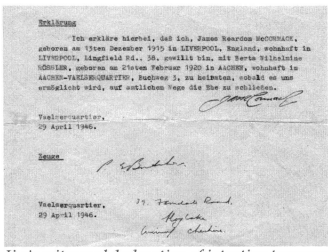

Jim's witnessed declaration of intention to marry

However, official channels evidently moved slowly, for by November seemingly not much progress had been made. On 3rd November – 95 letters later – he again urged her to be patient, no doubt aware of the reputation for gargantuan bureaucracy, red tape and incompetence which the Control Commission in Germany had developed. The visa for Britain could not be issued until permission was granted to leave Germany. But in the same letter he already explains that he has applied for a period of leave in December when he anticipates being able to come and collect her, planning by some means to meet her at the border with Holland. He also mentions a newspaper report he has read announcing five German girls' arrival in Britain to marry soldiers.

Not long after this, in November, Minny received notification to go to Düsseldorf, to be interviewed in German by a representative of the Military Government, who had the power to grant or refuse permission to leave Germany. In a bag she carried a certificate from Doctor Kremer, attesting good health, the statement from Jim, declaring in German he was willing to marry her as soon as legally possible, and the bundles of letters from him and his family received over previous months.

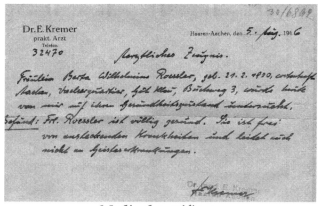

Medical certificate

Minny, full of trepidation, travelled by train to Düsseldorf and explained how she had spent the war years, her family background, and the details of her relationship with Jim, corroborating her story with the documents which she spread out on the desk of the British official. It was a long and searching interview. Suddenly the interviewer reached for a form, entered her details, stamped it and handed it to her. "Good luck to you", he said in English, "You are the first girl from *Nordrheinwestfalen* – North-Rhine Westphalia, the recently newly created state – to get one of these. Take care of it!" It was the permit to leave Germany and travel to England. Minny didn't understand "Take care of it", but as soon as she could, she hid in the toilet, and concealed the document in her underwear, where it would be safer than in a bag, should she be mugged on the way home!

By late autumn 1946, 64 FSS numbers had steadily decreased as personnel had been demobbed and repatriated to Britain. Captain Pennison had been one of the first to go, returning home after suffering injuries in a car accident. Paul too had left, leaving his German fiancée, Marianne, in Aachen. Border controls were now in the hands of the British Frontier Control Service, established in mid-1946 as part of the Control Commission and manned by British uniformed civilians working in conjunction with Dutch and Belgian officials. Minny and her family continued to live at Gut Klau but no longer enjoyed the privileges resulting from employment by the British. It was basic, sparse accommodation under the eaves of the house. Her mother slept in the bath, her brother had salvaged an old army-issue bedframe, which was pushed into the corner of the living area. Her father slept on a dilapidated sofa. At night she went to sleep at the house of a neighbour, who had a bed to spare.

Even after her documents had been issued, nothing was certain. Over the summer she had learned of a German lady who had worked in England before the war, who agreed to practise English conversation every week with Minny in return for cigarettes or groceries. At Berta and Emil's small wooden table she wrestled with the English language, writing long lists of vocabulary and verb parts in a notebook and even began to compose letters in faltering English on thin pale blue sheets of paper, which Jim sent back corrected! Winter set in.

Then one night in the first week of December, there was a knock at the door. It was Jim. He had not managed to send an advance message of his arrival. Eight months had elapsed since Jim's departure as a soldier, dressed in British Army uniform. He now came as a civilian, wearing the "demob" suit and overcoat issued to servicemen. Emil sat with Minny and discussed her predicament. Should she go with Jim or remain in Germany? Either scenario would involve difficulty and uncertainty. They deliberated into the night. Emil would consistently decline invitations to visit Minny in Britain, while Berta made the journey numerous times. But they did not try to persuade her one way or the other. It would certainly have been in their interests for her to stay. Minny wept with the frustration of indecision, but as her thoughts began to clear and she weighed up her position, her love for Jim overrode all other considerations.

The trunk, having survived air attacks and perilous journeys back and forth across the river Rhine in the final months of the war, as the Allied armies advanced across Europe, would now travel across the sea to Britain. Emil, well-travelled as a chauffeur, was skilled in the art of packing. He laid the Persian rug carefully on top of clothes, bed and table linen and eased the baize-lined lid into place, securing the straps and checking the clasps.   The next morning Minny departed with Jim.

Minny, 1946

CHAPTER NINE

1947: Assimilation

Minny understood little of their wedding ceremony on
13th December 1946, a mere week after arriving in
Liverpool. But almost immediately she became involved in
preparations for her first Christmas in Britain. Mother-in-law
Nora took her to the covered market where she had been a
regular customer throughout the war and where a trader had
promised to set aside a chicken on Christmas Eve. They were

too late; he had already left, and they returned home empty-handed.

Minny's overwhelming memory of the first Christmas in England is a growing and persistent feeling of homesickness. No phone connections enabled her to speak to her parents. Christmas lunch centred on a tinned ham, a gift from Jim senior's employer, who ran a company exporting canned goods.

Jim's brother, Tony, who was discharged from the RAF in the summer and was unable to attend the wedding, returned from London. During the train journey back to Liverpool, his suitcase had been stolen, leaving him with one set of clothes, in which he was standing. He immediately made Minny feel welcome, overcoming the lack of a common language with his friendly and easy-going nature. Nora urged Jim senior and Minny to "Speak English!" whenever they lapsed into German, so that family members could join in conversations.

Jim, Minny and Tony

After Christmas newly-wed Jim returned with Tony to London, where Jim had recently started work as a Customs and Excise officer. Although he had left school at 16, he had studied European languages from books, and as a natural scholar and linguist his inclination was to finish his higher education, going to university, building a career in teaching and research, reading medieval French Arthurian epics, filling notebooks with obscure vocabulary. But he was now married, with a new wife to support, who remained in Liverpool with his family.

Minny cannot recall ever being warm during the first winter, one of the coldest on record. The cold seemed damper, more penetrating than in Germany, forcing every family member to seek warmth from the only open fire in the house, in the dining room, in front of which bread was toasted on a long brass toasting fork. When everyone was in the room, a heavy curtain was drawn across a rail attached to the door, to conserve heat. The chilly formal sitting room was hardly ever entered.

Nora now set to work initiating Minny into British ways and, as Nora spoke no German, much of Minny's basic English was learned through demonstrations and sign language. "Here, Minny", Nora said, waving a duster, and making appropriate circular movements, "Dust!".

Nora got up early every morning to rake the ashes, light the fire and make tea. In Germany tea is mostly drunk with lemon, and soon Minny learned to appreciate the restorative qualities of tea with milk. In Liverpool she was introduced to salted butter, which was more palatable than the pungent German farm butter churned in large vats. Although Nora's father was Hungarian, she had never learned to cook the dishes of his native land and so Minny practised British pies and pastries, and tasted vegetables – swedes and turnips – which in Germany were normally fed to cattle. The thrift forced upon the population in the war was essential to feed a family, as food was still strictly rationed. Bread-and-butter pudding became a favourite.

From Germany Minny had brought a file of her mother's family recipes, typed on thick sheets of paper and using ingredients that would not be available for years to come. To this she added new recipes from Nora, whom she was already calling "Mother", such as Christmas cake and trifle. She cut out food tips from the newspaper, issued by the Ministry of Food, which used rationed ingredients. Nora and Jim senior had never tried to supplement their diet with home-grown produce, so Minny suggested digging over a patch of the small back garden and planting seeds for vegetables, a suggestion they followed as spring advanced.

Pages from Minny's recipe book

The only foods not rationed in the port of Liverpool were fish, a vital part in everyone's menus, and rabbit. Nora and Minny spent a large proportion of every day finding and buying provisions. When word got around that a shop had received a delivery, they took their places in long lines, waiting patiently with ration cards. In this activity at least Minny was well practised, although the orderliness of the queues was a surprise! Sometimes Nora left her in one queue and placed herself in another, to gain time. By the time Minny reached the front, she had rehearsed a few faltering words and handed over the coupons. An accent from abroad was no novelty in Liverpool. If shopkeepers and others noticed her hesitant English and strong accent, they didn't comment. The community into which she had moved was surely aware of her origins, but if hostility was expressed, she was unaware of it, unable to understand much of what she was hearing. Jim's family must have shielded her from many remarks.

When she began to meet the extended family members, however, there was clearly tension. Nora's brother Joe Golics and his wife Sis, short for Cecily, with their daughter Frances, visited Lingfield Road to meet her. Sis ignored Minny and refused to speak to her. Bizarrely Sis was also a first cousin of Jim McCormack senior. When not at work, he proudly showed Minny some of the sights of Liverpool, bomb-damaged though many still were, such as the Mersey tunnel, constructed in 1934 under the river. Liverpool had experienced its own Blitz in 1940, as German bombers sought to destroy the extensive dock areas to disrupt supplies arriving by sea.

From January 1947, Jim returned to Liverpool by train every weekend, eager to be reunited with Minny. Each Sunday evening she accompanied him to the train station, returning to Lingfield Road by tram. But at the first attempt, the tram stop where she had to get out by the cemetery wall looked unfamiliar in the dark and she rode on to the end of the line. Her English skills deserted her. The tram conductor realised she was lost, noted her accent and directed her onto the next tram back to the correct stop, where Jim senior was waiting anxiously under a street lamp. With him there was no language barrier: he was the only person with whom she had the mental release of being able to speak German, while husband Jim was absent in London. When Jim junior excitedly announced she could soon join him in rooms he had located to rent in Highgate, North London, she experienced mixed feelings.

The trunk, once again called upon to play its part, was packed with sheets, blankets, clothes, dishes, pans and the Persian rug, and was taken to the station for the journey to London. Soon after her 27th birthday, in February 1947, Jim and Minny moved into a first floor room at Number 5, Hornsey Lane Gardens, Highgate, London, a draughty three-storey Edwardian house, while Tony occupied a second room.

The company and support in Liverpool during Minny's first eventful weeks in Britain were now absent. Once Jim and Tony had left for work in central London, no one remained to share a conversation, ask for advice or explain words of English. Left to her own devices, she had to search out groceries to buy, negotiating a strange city in an unfamiliar tongue.

In their one room she cooked meals for three on a single gas ring, whose supply was intermittent. Water had to be carried up the stairs in leaky metal buckets, from a standpipe on the street. She bought her first kettle with a whistle – unknown in Germany where water was boiled in a pan.

The early morning sounds of a milk-float, accompanied by a rattling of bottles, was similarly new. At night mice crept out from behind the fireplace into the room and threw themselves into the buckets, drowning in the icy water. The Persian rug was laid on the bed for extra warmth, as the sash windows shook in the wind and let in chilly draughts. In the mornings the insides of the window panes were coated with a layer of frost.

Contact with Minny's family since arrival in England had been sparse, and the postal service erratic. There was a telephone in Lingfield Road, in Liverpool, but Gut Klau had no connection. How could she describe her difficulties in letters to Germany, aware of their own struggles over a winter unprecedented in its harshness? Newspaper reports in Britain informed readers of the plummeting temperatures and blanket of snow across most of the country, the worst for decades, and the widespread hunger and disease facing German civilians during those winter months. There, daily allotted rations were steadily decreasing and would continue to do so. For many, conditions were more extreme than during the years of war. The young and the elderly, weakened by the deprivations of war, perished in their thousands.

But soon after arrival in England she was able to support her family in a concrete and unexpected way. The publisher and humanitarian Victor Gollancz had in September 1945 founded the charity "Save Europe Now" through which food parcels could be sent to Germany to ease the critical food shortages. After visiting the British Zone in the autumn of 1946, he published "In Darkest Germany" in January 1947, in which he records his observations of the ongoing malnutrition suffered by the German people, which shocked him deeply.

Once a month Minny scraped together a parcel of specified items – tea, coffee, tinned and dried groceries, jars of fish paste – to send to Aachen, carefully wrapped in sturdy brown paper and tied up with string. In spite of their own shortages, some had even been donated by Nora in Liverpool.

Emil and Berta in Germany were moved by the gesture of solidarity from their former adversaries, although often parcels arrived damaged or broken into, after several weeks in transit.

On Berta's first visit to Britain, several years later, she would meet Nora and Jim face to face, and thank them for their kindness.

Soon Minny began to explore London through its Underground and bus networks. A small brown notebook, which still survives, contained instructions for reaching places by bus or Tube. It became a document of early life in England, recording new words and phrases mastered, household accounts, lists of spending, recipes, addresses and conversions of quantities and amounts. Jim wrote down the slang words used for the British currency: quid, bob, tanner, copper, the latter confusingly also denoting a policeman! Much space is devoted to the number of ration coupons needed for each commodity.

Minny's attempts at mastering English were a constant source of amusement to other family members. "Mother-in-law" became "mother-in-love". When she tried to get through to Jim at work by telephone, the operator told her he was engaged. "But he's already married!" she finally replied, confused.

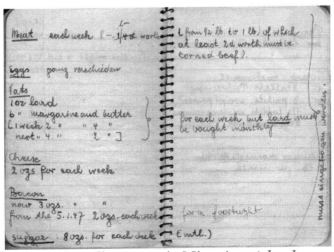

Ration allowances in Minny's notebook

Jim devised written exercises for Minny to improve her English, while at home they spoke a mixture of both languages, adding German verb endings to English words, such as "hoover" which became "hoovern".

Minny's English grammar book

Once a week Minny practised English at evening get-togethers arranged by Mrs Wood, the landlady, who owned several houses in the vicinity and rented rooms to ex-servicemen, who, like Jim and Tony, worked locally in London. Many had been RAF pilots, flying bombing raids over German cities. One evening Minny was shown an RAF log book – it recorded sorties over several towns in the vicinity of Aachen.

When Mrs Wood told her of a German-speaking doctor in the vicinity, she sat in a waiting room surrounded by graphic photographs on the walls. She does not recall previously having seen photos of Nazi atrocities committed in German concentration camps. The doctor's family had perished in the camps; in German he spoke with Minny about the Holocaust.

Minny's explorations of the London streets inevitably led to the Foreign Office, where she persistently sought clarification as to when a visit to Germany was permitted, or when family members could visit England. It would be another two and a half years before it became possible, in the autumn of 1949.

As the strains and uncertainties of the previous year took their toll, Minny suffered from fatigue and weight loss, so they travelled by train to Dartmouth in Devon on a delayed honeymoon. Jim was keen to show Minny new areas of the British Isles. They returned to the house where he had received bed and breakfast when his intelligence unit was stationed in Devon prior to D-Day, and he introduced Minny to his former landlady, Mrs Plowright, who supplemented food rations with produce from local farms. Spring flowers were more advanced than those in London. They walked by the sea, took boat trips on the river Dart and passed Slapton Sands, still cordoned off by barbed wire, where troops had practised for the D-Day landings and several hundred Allied lives had been lost through attack by German fast patrol boats; the incident, caused by poor coordination, was kept secret at the time. During the honeymoon, the song of the day was "Zippedy Doo-Dah" by the American singer Paul Robeson. Across the Dart estuary, Agatha Christie's house was visible on the hill. They returned to London refreshed and renewed.

But change was afoot. John Rees, a Reuters correspondent in Germany after the war, whom Jim knew from army days and who worked in Fleet Street, owned 3, Cooper Road, Hanwell, and made them an offer. Minny and Jim might move into his spare bedroom. In return would Minny manage the household and cook? After their return from Devon, the small but comfortable house became their new home.

Food rationing still dominated everyone's lives. But in Hanwell, a Sainsbury's grocers' shop had recently opened, where customers went from counter to counter, asking for each item individually. There was also a plentiful supply of unrationed rabbits for sixpence each – a source of nutritious stews.

When Jim McCormack senior visited them in Hanwell *en route* for Germany, Minny found it hard to comprehend that while he was permitted to visit Germany – seconded to the Control Commission at Bad Pyrmont as translator and interpreter, he would later be transported in an ageing shaking aeroplane to Berlin during the airlift of 1947-48 – she was still denied entry.

The pattern of Minny and Jim's early life was in many ways echoed by other German women who had ventured to Britain after the bans were relaxed. But each situation was unique, determined by random circumstances of location and, most crucially, personalities. Paul Butcher, also from Liverpool, also part of the 64 FSS Intelligence unit at Kaisersruh in 1945, married Marianne, whose family lived in Herzogenrath on the outskirts of Aachen, in March 1947.

Tony, Minny, Jim, Marianne and Paul

Like Jim, Paul worked in London for Customs and Excise, while Marianne stayed in Liverpool with his family. His father owned a men's outfitters and haberdashery business in Hoylake, a seaside resort near Liverpool, but his stepmother did not welcome Marianne. By then Minny had already moved to London, unable to offer support. Paul and Marianne too soon followed, occupying a small flat in one of the short narrow streets leading from the Strand to the Thames Embankment.

With Jim senior and Nora's help, Jim and Minny bought their first house, 179, Westbury Avenue, Southall, in the summer of 1948; Tony occupied the spare room. It was an arrangement beneficial to both parties. A small amount of extra income contributed to household costs and Tony was spared the laborious task of finding lodgings in post-war London.

Since moving to Britain, Minny had not come into contact with other Germans except Marianne. Now, in Westbury Avenue, the milkman mentioned in passing a German lady living in a nearby street. In the space of a week she met Lore, from Hannover, whom they referred to as "Singapore Lore" after her British husband was posted to the Far East, and Lia from Vienna, recently arrived in England with her husband August, a pioneering helicopter designer who worked in the fledgling British helicopter industry. The three became lifelong friends; their children would become playmates.

Minny and Lia

A photo shows Lia and Minny dressed in their best clothes, in Leicester Square, London. Each month they took ten shillings out of carefully husbanded housekeeping money, caught the Underground to central London and treated themselves to lunch in a Lyons Corner House. Minny bought a small treat for Jim at Fortnum and Mason. Some cash was always put aside towards the next outing. Britain was slowly emerging from the days of post-war gloom and austerity, although rationing would not be fully abolished until 1954. But a "New Look" in fashion hastened a sense of optimism. Lia, a talented seamstress, sewed and altered clothes to match the mood of the day. They heard of a warehouse in East London selling used parachute silk and sought it out. After the fine stitching had been laboriously unpicked, Lia sewed nightdresses and petticoats out of the pale, light and durable fabric. For entertainment they went to the cinema to watch Ealing comedies and warm up after the chill of the streets.

Many thousands of German prisoners-of-war were still held in camps in post-war Britain. Out of the blue Minny received a request from a former school friend in Aachen. Would Minny visit her brother, in such a camp at Hildenborough in Kent? She went in trepidation, not knowing what to expect. The last POWs would not be repatriated until 1949, some remaining in Britain and marrying British girls, a reverse of her own situation.

After Jim had written to the camp commandant requesting a visit, Herbert was permitted to meet them at the house of a pacifist family, who had befriended some of the German prisoners. Herbert expressed a wish to be able to see the sights of London, which was granted as long as Jim guaranteed his safe return. On the streets Herbert received shouts of abuse, as his status as a German POW was sewn in prominent letters on the back of his uniform.

Herbert and Jim in London

Jim wrote tirelessly to the Foreign Office, requesting permission for Erhard to visit Britain and Minny to travel to Germany. Minny and Jim finally returned to Aachen in September 1949. Bertha and Emil were living in a cramped apartment up several flights of stairs on the main road in Haaren, above the practice of Dr Kremer, for whom Emil still worked as a driver. Erhard was serving an apprenticeship with a forestry company dealing in timbers. Shortly after Minny's departure, in early 1947, a "Bizone" had been created from the American and British Zones, becoming part of the Federal Republic of West Germany when it came into existence in May 1949. The DDR (German Democratic Republic) was created from the former Soviet Zone. Germany was divided and would remain so until 1990.

In Aachen, the scars of conflict had by no means been eradicated. Roads remained unrepaired, collapsed and bombed buildings fenced off, until funds were available for clearance and repair; houses were pitted with bullet holes and gouges from shells. Decades later unexploded shells and bombs would periodically be found, and areas cordoned off so they might be safely defused. Roads and squares, which in the 1930s had been renamed after Nazi politicians, had regained their original designations, but it was more problematical to reverse the names of children christened "Adolf".

In post-war West Germany, the *Wirtschaftswunder* – economic miracle – as the state was rebuilt physically and economically, was accompanied by a growing process of *Vergangenheitsbewältigung* (coming to terms with the past, dealing with the past), which took on changing characteristics in each decade and for each generation. It gained further dimensions after the reunification of a divided Germany. Those in the Communist DDR gained the freedom to reflect openly both on roles and lives under that regime, and on a more distant Third Reich past, experiencing what was sometimes termed a *doppelte Vergangenheitsbewältigung* – a double dealing with the past.

Minny's first return to Germany set a pattern for future years. Every summer she and Jim travelled by sea and train, accompanied by the trunk, now provided with new luggage labels pasted over ageing remains of previous ones. Each flaking layer represented a phase of the trunk's history. Jim again marvelled at the interior of Charlemagne's cathedral, still standing defiantly against the skyline. Mirroring his first encounter with Minny' family, when he had knocked in 1945 requesting hot water for tea, he carried packets of tea to Aachen and tried in vain to replicate the taste of his "cuppa" abroad, discussing heatedly with an uncomprehending Berta why variations in water, milk, teacups and teapot meant it could never match up! Together with Minny he walked in the park at Kaisersruh where the large estate house stood empty and shuttered.

Herr Nellessen, whose family had been the original owners of the trunk, had died in 1948. Before she left Germany in 1946, he had formally presented Minny with his wife's engagement ring. They had no children, he explained carefully, and both wished the ring to serve as a reminder of childhood on their estate. In the spring of 1951, when Minny's and Jim's daughter was born in Britain, they received a parcel from Frau Nellessen of delicately crocheted clothes for the new baby, who was named Ingrid Wilhelmine McCormack, a name reflecting a dual and somewhat ambiguous heritage.

Ingrid

Jim, Minny and Ingrid moved to Surrey in the outer suburbs of London in 1955. Jim died of a brain tumour in 1972, shortly before Ingrid married an RAF pilot, whose professional predecessors had participated in the destruction of Germany from the air. Minny remained in the same house until the age of 94, moving to the countryside on the day before her 95th birthday. Sixty years of residence in one location to a great extent accounts for the preservation of much documentary material from the 1940s.

The story of Jim and his German bride is not unique. It is estimated that about 10,000 British servicemen and ex-servicemen married German women in the months after the ban was relaxed in the summer of 1946, and settled down to life in post-war Britain.

For Minny and Jim, the long shadow of the war would occasionally reappear to remind them of the unusual circumstances under which they had met. In the early 1960s, on holiday in Bavaria, they took a boat ride on the Chiemsee, a lake surrounded by picturesque mountains and alpine-style villages. Minny became aware that a man was fixing his gaze on her. As he crossed the deck of the boat to talk to her, recognition dawned. It was a colleague from the police station in Aachen, Waldemar, who had been reported missing in the slaughter at Stalingrad in 1941. "But I thought you were dead", she managed to say. There was much history to relate. Jim became increasingly agitated as he observed a stranger talking to his wife in a seemingly intimate manner. *"Wer war dieser Mann?"* (Who was that man?) asked Ingrid as they disembarked.

Waldemar had been captured in Russia and only released with the final waves of prisoners repatriated in the late 1950s. Stalin's government regarded the use of German prisoners in labour camps as a legitimate component of Germany's war reparations to the Soviet Union. Thousands perished in the harsh conditions. Jim's mind was put at rest with an introduction and explanation. Waldemar, one of the millions of victims damaged and scarred by war, had survived, to attempt to build a new life in post-war Germany. Minny too was one of the fortunate, a fact for which she today gives thanks.

In the 21st Century, as the number of those with personal experience of the post-war Anglo-German encounter is dwindling, it is imperative to document their perspectives on 20th Century history and acknowledge a singular contribution to the richness of the historical record.

Postscript: Ingrid, 2016

As a child in the 1950s, visiting my grandparents Emil and Berta at 1, Hauptstrasse, Haaren, I perched on a small wooden stool and peered out of the tiny window of their eaves apartment to watch the rise and fall of the level crossing barrier far below on the street and the trains rumbling slowly past towards Aachen's main railway station. *"Warum"*, I asked my father later, as we walked through the city streets, *"ist alles kaputt?"* – "Why is everything in ruins"? It would be many decades before I began to understand the reasons.

There was never a time when the German language was not part of my conscious thought. When starting primary school in the London suburbs in 1956, I barely spoke English. Many so-called German "war brides" and their British husbands understandably did not raise children in bilingual homes. But Jim my father was a linguist. Berta and Emil, my grandparents, spoke no English and never attempted to learn. *"Das Kind"*, Berta announced *"muss Deutsch lernen"* (the child is to learn German).

Circumstances often do not seem out of the ordinary until they are considered with hindsight. Now I realise how my life's experiences were fed by two cultures which to me flowed together seamlessly, but to others embodied irreconcilable enmities. Many of the playthings and books stacked in the cupboard of the room overlooking a neat British suburban garden are today collectors' items: dark cautionary tales of *Struwelpeter* and *Max und Moritz*, Steiff animals, delicately crafted German dolls and dolls-house furniture.

Ingrid with German toy "Mecki"

In Advent, parcels of home-baked biscuits arrived, filling the kitchen with pungent scents of cinnamon and cloves, and protected by hand-made oven cloths and cardigans. Our Christmas tree was illuminated with wax candles balanced in wobbly metal clips which singed the branches. We shared holidays and outings with couples where one or both partners were German speakers, whose children, like me, expressed themselves in a mixture of the two languages and were fed on foods from two culinary traditions.

Gathering of German-speaking families in London

Living with dual perspectives brings its problems. Patriotism is a difficult emotion. I am neither fully German nor fully British, cheering for neither side in Norman Tebbitt's "cricket test" of allegiances, loving the "Last Night of the Proms" musically but feeling distinctly uncomfortable with sentiments embodied in the phrase "How shall we extol thee, who are born of thee?" from "Land of Hope and Glory", which year by year never fails to raise unanswerable questions in my mind. A natural inner detachment that comes from being an only child is exacerbated by another isolation of identity.

By the time as an adult I began to research the story of the trunk, many of those whose lives were bound up with its history were no longer alive. My father Jim died shortly before I married, but not before he had by sheer hard work and determination gained a PhD in Medieval French Literature at Birkbeck College, London, while working full-time as a civil

servant. Grandfather Emil died in his sleep when I was barely
a teenager. If only I could have talked to him of Istanbul,
Damascus, Aleppo. Once he slipped a heavy silver Turkish
coin into my childish hand as a gift. It was probably one of the
few tangible reminders of his secondment to the Turkish Army
in 1916. I still have it.

*Four generations: the author, her grandmother, mother and
daughter*

But Berta his wife, my grandmother, lived to be 103. In the
early stages of my research over 20 years ago, she still lived in
Haaren on the outskirts of Aachen, still walked miles out of her
way to save a few Pfennigs on special offers for groceries, still
talked wistfully of Kaisersruh. When I tentatively inquired
about reactions to her daughter marrying an Englishman, she
paused before answering. "We had nothing against him
personally" she finally said. As a child the sight of Berta's hand
with a thumb missing both repelled and fascinated me. It
represented something I did not yet understand. She visited
my parents on numerous occasions in England, while Emil
refused all invitations, claiming he could not face the sea

journey. Maybe he was physically frailer than he cared to admit, having returned from service as a soldier in Palestine in the First World War suffering from malaria, whose sporadic after-effects were felt until his death.

My paternal grandmother Nora died when I was only six. How would she have answered my questions about Minny's first weeks in England? Both her and Jim senior's letters to my mother reveal people with exceptional qualities. Grandfather Jim outlived her by many years, punctuating his speech with pithy German and English phrases.

As I write, I am surrounded by objects from the everyday lives of all four grandparents. From Nora and Jim I have books, notebooks, letters, jewellery and kitchen utensils. From Berta and Emil there are rings, household equipment that survived British bombs and the gold chain to Emil's pocket watch.

Today, the estate house at Kaisersruh is a precarious ruin, its roof caved in, the once elegant rooms open to the elements. Surrounded by protective fencing and shored up with numerous metal struts to prevent total collapse, it is a listed building whose demolition is not permitted. Many schemes for its resurrection over the past two decades have come to nothing, but a further scheme for restoration and renovation is currently at the planning stage and has received wide coverage in the local press. The decaying former Rössler family house in its shadow is similarly listed, cordoned off, and part of the planned restoration. Residents of Aachen now have access to the parkland and wooded areas for cycling and walking.

One element of the former estate, though, is still inhabited and functioning: the Zintzen farm from where Wilhelm Zintzen, who as a child fled Aachen on a farm cart in 1944 with my grandmother Berta and the trunk, now operates riding stables with his wife Maria. As a child on holidays in Aachen, I clearly recall afternoon visits to his mother, Frau Zintzen senior, who served boiled eggs at a huge wooden kitchen table. The taste of freshly collected farm eggs was unlike anything I had ever experienced.

As Aachen and its transport links have grown, the road from the city, once flanked by few houses, has been widened so that the Kaisersruh estate is no longer reached along a drive, but stands a few yards from the busy road, surrounded by motorway access lanes and constant thundering traffic.

The author surveys the ruins of Kaisersruh, 2016

At the border in Vaalserquartier, the customs house where Jim and his colleagues worked has been demolished. The transition from Germany to Holland is indicated by a simple sign, as people, goods and vehicles now move freely across the national boundaries. The unique position of Aachen at a crossroads of cultures and languages, coupled with its 20th Century history, led the city to establish the *Karlspreis* – Charlemagne Prize – in 1950, awarded annually to a person who has made a significant contribution to European cohesion and unification. Recipients have included Winston Churchill and Edward Heath.

Today Minny lives surrounded by images of Aachen, its cathedral and streets, and the oak tree at Kaisersruh with plaque documenting the origins of its name. Denied seeing Berlin in September 1939, she finally visited in 2000 when I was living and working in that city.

The trunk accompanied me to Berlin, once again filled with clothes and bedding, returning to the country of its manufacture. Now, flanked by the Persian rug, it sits in my home, an ordinary piece of luggage with an extraordinary history.

Historical Notes

Note 1

The Control Commission for Germany (British Element) – CCG/BE– was set up to support the Military Government and assumed full authority for the British Zone on 3rd September 1945. It issued a series of directives over the following years establishing policy, the first of which appeared on 10th September 1945. Junior British government minister John Hynd was appointed head of the Control Commission in October 1945. Headquarters of Montgomery's BAOR (British Army of the Rhine) were established in Bad Oeynhausen, in Westphalia, and Control Commission departments moved into undamaged buildings in nearby towns. Eventually the Military Government was phased out and the Control Commission took over.

Note 2

See *die Zeit*, 29th June 2007, *Mitglied ohne Beitritt* ("Membership without Application") and *die Welt*, 1st July 2007, *Gab es Kollektivaufnahmen in die NSDAP?* ("Were people collectively enrolled into the NSDAP?").

Note 3

Field Security (FS) Duties

(Source: Manual of Field Security, 1943):

Tasks included:

- Compiling and using Black and White Lists from information provided from multiple sources including the Secret Intelligence Service (SIS), Special Operations Executive (SOE), and Ultra. Black Lists were for the arrest of known enemy intelligence operatives and sympathisers/ collaborators. White Lists were used for contact with local resistance and friendly persons.
- Arrest and Field Interrogation of Black List/high category prisoners such as the SS, Gestapo, the SD, local Nazis/sympathizers (Intelligence Corps personnel were often selected for language skills).
- Searching of captured enemy HQ/Intelligence offices, etc for valuable intelligence information and translation of documents.
- Briefing Division and Brigade intelligence staff officers with information derived from the above.
- Key point security and security investigations prior to operational deployment.

Field Security Section (FSS) units were deployed with the British Army wherever it operated, successively in North Africa, Italy, France, the Low Countries, Germany and Austria, and the Far East. They operated normally at Brigade to Division level and usually at the forward edge of advance.

Operationally, the FSS were responsible to the formation HQ General Staff Officers - GSO 2 (Int) - working with the GSO 3 (Int). For technical and policy issues, FSS were responsible to HQ Intelligence Corps (Field). For domestic issues, the parent formation was responsible for things such as: accommodation, equipment, communications, feeding, etc.

Note 4

The Potsdam Conference at the end of July and beginning of August specified the tasks of the Control Council, which constituted itself on 30th August and issued its first proclamation, informing the German people of its existence and that the commands and directives issued by the commanders-in-chief of each zone would not be affected by the establishment of the Council. France was not present at Potsdam, but participated in the council, in which the four nations were represented by Montgomery (Britain), Zhukov (Soviet Union), Eisenhower (USA) and Koenig (France), who had all been active commanders in the field. Berlin was to be divided into four zones, each controlled by a victorious power.

The text of the Potsdam protocol, which was to be the basis of Allied policies, is reproduced in the appendix to "Berlin Twilight", Lt. Col. W. Byford-Jones (see Bibliography)

The Allied Control Council (*Alliierter Kontrollrat*) was the overall governing body of the four-powers' military occupation, consisting of representatives of the victorious powers - Britain, the USA, France and the Soviet Union - and based in Berlin. It made unanimous decisions affecting Germany as a whole, while each power individually governed its own zone of occupation. On 5th June 1945 the four powers made a statement informing the German people of the control machinery to be set up in Germany.

Note 5

21st Army Group Counter-Intelligence Instruction No. 4: The Occupation of Germany (1944) (National Archives, Kew, WO

205/1086) lists the planned policies on policing the borders of Germany after its defeat as follows:

> "517. The detailed responsibilities of Frontier CI Sections include:
>
> (a) the implementation of travel control policy as laid down by SHAEF (Supreme Headquarters Allied Expeditionary Force)/Control Commission;
>
> (b) the coordination of measures designed to prevent the illegal crossing of the frontier;
>
> (c) checking of all travellers and the enforcement at the frontier of travel permit regulations and censorship regulations insofar as they apply to travellers;
>
> (d) making preliminary investigations into and interrogating doubtful and undocumented travellers and persons attempting to cross the frontier without authority;
>
> (e) sending suspects to internment camps for further investigation;
>
> (f) the security control of Displaced Persons. In this matter close liaison will be maintained with Mil Gov Border Control Stations
>
> (g) making local arrangements for the security control of frontiers;
>
> (h) organising security patrols and snap checks on possible unauthorised routes and giving advice to the local military commander as to the disposition of AEF frontier guards."

Note 6

Each of the four occupying powers would come to interpret and implement denazification policies differently in their own zones. In the British Zone, on the basis of information noted in questionnaires, citizens wishing to be re-employed in official and government posts under the new order would be classified into one of five categories signifying degrees of collaboration with the previous regime: *"Hauptschuldige"*, (major offenders) *"Belastete"*, (offenders, activists) *"Minderbelastete"*, (lesser offenders) *"Mitläufer"*, (followers) and *"Entlastete"* (exonerated). Those in the highest categories were denied roles in the reconstruction of Germany and barred from certain jobs. It was considered important that a more thorough "purge" was required in professions such as the justice system and education. The most coveted classification was one leading to the issue of what became known as a *Persilschein* (Persil certificate), clearing the recipient of involvement and ensuring the possibility of a clean start in most job spheres.

But the sheer volume of people to be processed and the unworkability of making a clean sweep in all spheres led to controversy and compromise. A blind eye was frequently turned in the interests of making use of minor offenders' valuable skills and insights in helping to build new administrative structures.

Denazification policies and categories were defined and implemented through a series of Directives issued by the Control Commission Germany (CCG) starting in late 1945 and continuing throughout 1946-8. The most significant of these was issued on 5th September 1945 on the "Arrest, Removal and Exclusion of Nazis from Office". Later Directives would redefine and extend criteria. But in the months after total capitulation, thousands of suspects were taken into custody, pending investigations, without any clear idea of what was to be their fate. Conditions under which internees lived were generally appalling and caused debate in both Britain and Germany. Thousands died in internment, where hardships and brutalities often far exceeded those experienced during the Nazi regime.

Note 7

Excellent accounts of differing aspects of the British occupation zone in Germany are to be found in: Christopher Knowles' unpublished thesis of 2015, *Winning the Peace*, focusing on biographies of people tasked with the rebuilding of Germany; Patricia Meehan's *A Strange Enemy People* and *Conditions of Surrender: Britons and Germans witness the end of the war* edited by Ulrike Jordan. (See Bibliography for details).

Acknowledgements

The story of the trunk and its owners has been compiled over the course of more than two decades. I am greatly indebted to all those who have contributed to, enhanced and verified the disparate strands of the narrative. In Britain, Minny McCormack, Tony McCormack and Thea Dunnage, née McCormack, have been both generous and honest in their recollections. Tony's written account of his family history is lucid and fascinating. On the German side, Erhard Rössler has filled in many details about Aachen and the war, and has patiently answered questions. Anita Deutz, *née* Kreuz, before she passed away, and her daughter Irene Ottenhausen have provided me with war diaries, recollections and anecdotes. Wilhelm Zintzen, who as a child was evacuated from the Kaisersruh estate, along with my grandmother, to his grandparents in Gey, has kindly shared his memories of 1944 and 1945. Paul and Marianne Butcher emigrated from Britain to Australia in the 1970s, from where in the early stages of my enquiries Paul sent a penetrating account of the work of 64 FSS in Aachen in 1945. They are both now deceased.

A biography which is largely based on personal memoir has of course had to be painstakingly substantiated and cross-referenced by documentary evidence present in archives, and in the wealth of written academic and military research material available. I am indebted to archivists at the Intelligence Corps archive, especially A.F. Judge, and at the National Archives at Kew, as well as at the *Bundesarchiv* in Berlin and the *Stadtarchive* in Aachen and Würselen. Sheila Youngs, *née* Hynd, has shared documents from her research into her father, J.B. Hynd, appointed to head the British Control Commission in 1945.

I am particularly grateful to have received encouragement and written endorsements from Dr Philip Towle, Professor Peter Wilson and Jackie Ashley. Philip has given insightful, practical advice throughout the editing process. My connection with Lucy Cavendish College, where Jackie is President, is always an inspiration. Peter took a chance in agreeing to cast an expert eye over the narrative and his critical historical view has been extremely valuable.

Rosemary and Andrew Kingston and Julia and David Hardie have assisted with proofreading. Julia's book group in Cheltenham kindly agreed to read and comment on a first draft and confirmed my intention to write a second draft for a wider readership beyond immediate family members.

I am especially indebted to my family. My children and their spouses have commented on the narrative and its content. James Morgan has been a patient graphic artist, creating the logo, maps and cover designs. Special thanks are due to Tony's son, Steve McCormack, my cousin, and his wife Debbie, for proof-reading and suggesting changes at different stages. Most of all I thank my husband Peter for his extensive and time-consuming technical input and patience. When we met, he did not suspect he would be confronted with a new language, different traditions and a controversial period of recent history.

Select Bibliography

History of Germany in Second World War and aftermath

Beevor, Antony, *Ardennes 1944, Hitler's last Gamble,* Viking, 2015

Evans, Richard J., *The Third Reich in History and Memory,* Little Brown, 2015

Evans, Richard J., *The Third Reich in Power,* Penguin, 2006

Gollancz, Victor, *In Darkest Germany,* Henry Regnery Co, Hinsdale IL, 1947

Hastings, Max, *The Secret War, Spies, Codes and Guerillas, 1939-45,* HarperCollins UK, 2015

Hoffman, Moritz, *Als der Krieg nach Hause kam,* Propyläen, Berlin, 2015

Kershaw, Ian, *To Hell and Back,* Viking, 2015

Krockow, Christian, *The hour of the women,* Faber and Faber, London, 1992

Stargardt, Nicholas, *The German War, A Nation under Arms, 1939-45,* Penguin Random House, 2015

Van der Bijl, Nick, *Sharing the Secret, The History of the Intelligence Corps 1940-2010,* Pen and Sword Military, 2015

History of Aachen, Battle of Aachen, post-war administrations in Aachen

Bürgerstiftung *Lebensraum Aachen, 70 Jahre Frieden und Freiheit in Aachen,* Meyer & Meyer Verlag, Aachen 2015

Küsters, Franz Joseph, *Der Zweite Weltkrieg zwischen Maas und Rur,* Meyer & Meyer Verlag, Aachen 1995

Siemons, Hans, *Off Limits, Alliierte Besatzung 1944 bis 1947 im Raum Aachen*, Meyer & Meyer Verlag, Aachen, 1994

Siemons, Hans, *Kriegsalltag in Aachen*, Meyer & Meyer Verlag, Aachen, 1998

Whiting, Charles, *Bloody Aachen*, Stein and Day, New York, 1976

Postwar Allied Occupation of Germany

Annan, Noel, *Changing enemies, the defeat and regeneration of Germany*, Harper Collins, London, 1995

Bacque, James, *Crimes and Mercies, the fate of German civilians under Allied occupation*, Little, Brown and Company, London, 1997

Byford-Jones, W. *Berlin Twilight*, Hutchinson and Co, 1947

Donnison, F.S.V., *Civil Affairs and Military Government Northwest Europe 1944-1946*, Her Majesty's Stationery Office, London 1961

Jordan, Ulrike, ed., *Conditions of surrender: Britons and Germans witness the end of the War*, I.B. Tauris, London (German Historical Institute)

Knowles, Christopher, *Winning the Peace*, University of London unpublished PhD thesis, 2015

Macdonogh, Giles, *After the Reich*, John Murray, London, 2007

Meehan, Patricia, *A Strange Enemy People, Germans under the British 1945-50*, Peter Owen Publishers, London, 2001

Smith, Barbara, *The Rules of Engagement, German Women and British Occupiers, 1945-9*, Online Dissertation, Wilfrid Laurier University, 2009

Trees, Wolfgang, Whiting, Charles and Omansen, Thomas, *Drei Jahre nach Null, Geschichte der britischen Besatzungszone 1945-48*, Droste Verlag, Düsseldorf, 1978

THE AUTHOR

The author in Aachen, 2016

Ingrid Dixon studied German and Italian at the University of
Bristol, education at the University of Cambridge and art
history at the Courtauld Institute in London. She has written
teaching material and taught German and academic English at
the University of Cambridge. Her MA research on a 14th
Century Italian altarpiece, brought to Britain by Victorian
architect George Edmund Street, architect of the London Law
Courts, has been published in Italy. She and her husband have
two adult children and four young grandchildren.

52464171R00124

Made in the USA
Columbia, SC
03 March 2019